CALDERÓN

THE PHYSICIAN OF HIS HONOUR

EL MÉDICO DE SU HONRA

INGENS FAMA, SED
ALTERIVS EA EST IGEPS

Resplendence of the Spanish Monarchy: Renaissance Tapestries and Armor from the Patrimonio Nacional (Metropolitan Museum of Art)

ARIS & PHILLIPS HISPANIC CLASSICS

PEDRO CALDERÓN DE LA BARCA

The Physician of His Honour

El médico de su honra

Translated with an Introduction, Notes, and Appendix
by

Dian Fox with Donald Hindley

Second Edition
by

Dian Fox

Aris & Phillips is an imprint of Oxbow Books

Published in the United Kingdom by
OXBOW BOOKS
10 Hythe Bridge Street, Oxford OX1 2EW

and in the United States by
OXBOW BOOKS
908 Darby Road, Havertown, PA 19083

Paperback Edition: ISBN 978-0-85668-777-8

A CIP record for this book is available from the British Library

For a complete list of Aris & Phillips titles, please contact:

UNITED KINGDOM
Oxbow Books
Telephone (01865) 241249
Fax (01865) 794449
Email: oxbow@oxbowbooks.com
www.oxbowbooks.com

UNITED STATES OF AMERICA
Oxbow Books
Telephone (800) 791-9354
Fax (610) 853-9146
Email: queries@casemateacademic.com
www.casemateacademic.com/oxbow

Oxbow Books is part of the Casemate Group

Printed and bound by CPI Group (UK) Ltd, Croydon, CR0 4YY

Front cover: Body floating in fiery pool, *And Images,* © *Getty Images*

For Katie
and her grandparents

CONTENTS

Revised Introduction

THE PLAYWRIGHT

Don Pedro Calderón de la Barca was born in Madrid in 1600. We know that his father intended him to enter the priesthood in the Catholic Church. Calderón received early training with the Jesuits, but after his father's death veered away from the religious trajectory for a time. His gifts for poetry and drama won acclaim during the 1620s, and Calderón was in the prime of life when the great Lope de Vega died in 1635. Although Calderón's *The Physician of His Honour* was first published in 1637, it has been suggested that it was performed as early as 1628 or 1629.[1] Recognized and rewarded by King Philip IV for his accomplishments in theatre, in the 1630s Calderón was appointed Court Dramatist and Knight of the Order of Santiago. He served with the military and retired after being wounded in a 1642 campaign in Catalonia. He continued to write not only comedies and tragedies, but also religious plays, refining the one-act *auto sacramental*, intended to be performed at the yearly Corpus Christi celebrations. In 1651, never having married but finally fulfilling his father's wishes, Calderón took holy orders. He continued to write until his death in 1681. In the later period of his life Calderón tended to devote his pen to religious theatre and to mythological plays designed for court consumption.[2]

THE *COMEDIA*

Calderón was a master of the *comedia*. The term refers to any three-act play, in verse, written during Spain's Golden Age – that is, the brilliant sixteenth and seventeenth centuries. A *comedia* can be comic or tragic. While the most

---

1   Shergold and Varey (1961, p. 281) found records of palace performances in 1628 or 1629 that could be referring to the original *The Physician of His Honour*, which served as a source of Calderón's play and has sometimes been attributed to Lope de Vega.
2   For a more detailed summary of Calderón's life, see Cruickshank and Page, 'Introduction' to their edition and translation of *Love Is No Laughing Matter (No hay burlas con el amor)*, pp. vii–xiv.

famous of these plays were composed during the first half of the seventeenth century by Lope de Vega (1562–1635), Tirso de Molina (1580?–1648), and Calderón, numerous other dramatists wrote plays that continue to be read and performed today.

THE *DRAMA DE HONOR*

The Physician of His Honour is what is commonly called a *drama de honor*, an honour drama. This type of *comedia* has been much discussed by literary scholars attempting to come to terms with attitudes in these plays that make the condition of one's honour (meaning both 'reputation' and 'integrity') a central issue.[3] Donald R. Larson defines the 'honour play' in general terms as an ' "action" whose object is to regain "honour" that has been lost through an offense of some sort' (p. 1). Yvonne Yarbro-Bejarano narrows the definition to a drama 'in which the husband believes in the existence of a rival pursuing his wife' (p. 1). A man's belief in the existence of a rival is sufficient to damage his honour, which must then be repaired – often, in the *drama de honor*, in a most violent way.[4] In 1609 Lope de Vega, who during his lifetime composed several dozen *dramas de honor* (see Yarbro-Bejarano), offers a reason for their appeal: 'The subjects in which honour has a part' are good grist for the pen of the playwright, he explains, 'since they deeply stir everybody' (*New Art of Writing Plays*, 35) (Los casos de la honra son mejores, / porque mueven con fuerza a toda gente [*Arte nuevo de hacer comedias*, 163]).

In Calderón's three honour dramas, *Secret Wrong, Secret Revenge* (*A secreto agravio, secreta venganza*), *The Painter of His Dishonour* (*El pintor de su deshonra*) and *The Physician of His Honour*, the husband's rival is a man who returns after a lengthy absence to find that his beloved has married. The rival sets his sights on the wife despite her resistance, his pursuit arousing the husband's suspicions. Once the husband's honour has been compromised by the pursuit, he becomes convinced that the dishonour can only be effaced with the deaths of the 'guilty' parties – that is, his wife and her suitor. Secrecy in the revenge is vital, since a man would not want

---

3   On the two Spanish words for honour used in *The Physician – honor* and *honra* – see the Appendix.
4   Many of these plays also fall into the category of the 'wife-murder *comedias*'. See Stroud.

to publicise an injury done to him, thus further damaging his honour. In the case of the present play, the husband Don Gutierre imagines himself 'physician' to his ailing honour.[5] Because his rival happens to be a member of the royal family – Prince Enrique, bastard half-brother to King Pedro – the offended husband exempts the pursuer from revenge and 'cures' his honour by turning solely on the wife.

Such a recourse would be potentially dramatic enough, but in Calderón's honour dramas the husbands murder wives who have remained faithful.[6] To compound the shock – to the modern reader or spectator, certainly, and no doubt also to the 'deeply stirred' contemporary playgoer[7] – the works conclude with the approval of the murders by the reigning figures of authority. In fact, *The Physician of His Honour* presents two honour conflicts, both intimately involving Don Gutierre, the resolution of both made possible with the murder of one woman. The astonishing finale of this play – the last 80 lines in the wake of the discovery to the King of the wife's corpse – has helped to bring *The Physician* and its author both fame and infamy in the centuries since the *comedia*'s composition. At the same time that King Pedro essentially condones Doña Mencía's death, he punishes the murderer in such a way that resolves the second honour conflict. The widower will have to marry Doña Leonor, whose honour he offended before the beginning of the play and who is fully aware of her new husband's bloody physic.

STRUCTURE

Lope de Vega had advised dramatists, 'In the first Act set forth the case, in the second weave together the events, in such wise that until the middle of the third Act one may hardly guess the outcome' (*New Art of Writing Plays*, p. 34). This traditional division by the playwright into three acts imposes a

---

5 See 'The Metaphor', below.
6 Although in *Secret Wrong* the wife's resolve wears thin in the face of the rival's persistence, and the pair are killed before they can carry out a planned tryst.
7 While we have no records describing the reception of *The Physician* in the seventeenth century, Calderón through his protagonist advises his audience to expect in the final scene something which will arouse great pity and fear. Gutierre sets the stage for the King and implicitly, for the public: 'listen to the strangest tragedy: the most extraordinary and astonishing thing has happened…. Turn your gaze in this direction, and you'll see the sun bloodied, you'll see the moon eclipsed, the stars drained of light, and the spheres obliterated. You'll see the saddest and most wretched beauty …' (2822–5, 2863–9). On the arousal of wonder (or *admiración*) in the play, see Wardropper (1958) p. 5.

certain rhythm on the action, of which Calderón takes full advantage. By the end of *The Physician*'s first act we have met all the major characters, and we learn of two past romantic links, now broken: that of Doña Mencía and Prince Enrique; and that of Don Gutierre and Doña Leonor. In the second act, the Prince's renewed pursuit of Mencía (and Gutierre's concomitant dishonour) becomes evident to the protagonist. In the third act, we see the ways in which Gutierre deals with his dilemma, but the results of his stratagems are not evident until the closing lines of the play.

A symmetry typical of Calderón informs the structure of *The Physician*. For example, the first and second acts open by bringing Prince Enrique to Doña Mencía's door; the third with Don Gutierre at the King's door to lodge his complaint. Doña Leonor closes the first act wishing in a violent apostrophe to Gutierre,[8] '...may you come to see your own dishonours, bathed in your blood' (1014–6), and she ends the third act accepting the same man's hand in marriage, knowing that 'it comes bathed in blood' (2943–4).

CHARACTERS

The Physician of His Honour is recognized as one of Calderón's finest – and most perplexing – *comedias*. The main characters are compelling and, like real people, contradictory in ways that bring them to life with both a clarity and an ambiguity that are startling.

King Pedro

The monarch who presides over the *deus-ex-machina* resolution is a strong presence throughout *The Physician of His Honour*: the life of each character in the play is altered by his judgments. Although 'he doesn't waste any words' (681),[9] King Pedro gives the impression of depth and complexity. At the beginning of the play, he seems driven by his sense of duty. When his brother the Prince falls in the opening scene, he expresses dismay: 'If this is the way he greets the towers of Seville, I wish he [or I][10] had never come! Better never to have left Castile! Enrique! Brother!' (5–9). Nevertheless, he leaves Enrique in the care of others as he goes on to the city where, apparently, business of state awaits. Pedro is generous throughout the play to supplicants, including

---

8   There is actually enough ambiguity in the apostrophe that it could be construed as addressing the King.

9   See 'Language and Style', below.

10 The Spanish is ambiguous here; see line 7 note.

those of low social rank. As he tells an old man to whom he has presented a diamond, 'Don't be surprised. I wish the whole world were a diamond that I could give you' (591–3). King Pedro takes very seriously the honour-related complaints of Doña Leonor and Don Gutierre. Called 'the Enforcer of Justice' (*el Justiciero*[11]) by Leonor (609), he views himself as 'an Atlas:[12] the entire weight of the law rests on my shoulders' (675–6). However, for the serious crime of *lèse majesté* Don Arias and Don Gutierre are not executed, but shortly pardoned, and when an even worse offense occurs – the King believes himself physically attacked by his brother – Pedro allows Enrique to go into exile. In Act Three, the monarch is clearly moved by the story of a woman's death, privately related to him by Ludovico. His companion Don Diego observes, 'Something has left you sad' (2714).

King Pedro, from a statue in the Museo Arqueológico Nacional, Madrid, with kind permission

---

11   On the translation of *el Justiciero*, see note 23 below.
12   On Atlas, see Frontispiece and line 675 note.

On the other hand, in the play Pedro has a reputation for harshness, and is viewed by his own courtiers as dangerous. In the opening scene when Pedro leaves his injured brother, Don Arias complains of the King's 'brutality' (27). Diego responds with a warning to his companion about the risk of voicing such criticism: 'Be quiet! Don't forget, Don Arias: if walls have ears, the trees have eyes, and nothing's safe for us' (32–5). The clown Coquín, forced by the King into a wager involving laughter and teeth, makes more than one reference to the monarch as severe and frightening.[13]

Pedro's most cryptic judgment occurs as the play reaches its dénouement. Confirming that Gutierre has murdered Mencía, the King gives his endorsement in the name of honour. He then compels the protagonist to take Leonor as his wife, a decision providing Leonor with the justice she has sought, and the play with its stunning conclusion.

Prince Enrique

Rival to Don Gutierre and half-brother to the King, Enrique had been in love with Doña Mencía before the beginning of the play. Returning to Seville after a long absence, he begins *The Physician of His Honour* with a bad fall from his horse, by chance outside Gutierre's country home. When the Prince recovers consciousness and finds that he is in the presence of Mencía (now married), he quickly determines to win her, despite all obstacles. Like the doomed rivals in Calderón's other *dramas de honor*, Prince Enrique foresees his own death (243–5, 274–5, 356–7), and pursues Mencía in utter disregard of her and her husband's honour.

While Enrique's means of pursuit are coolly premeditated, he is susceptible to panic: so much so that twice in the play he drops his dagger in highly incriminating circumstances. Surprised during his attempt on Mencía's honour early in Act Two by the return of Gutierre, the Prince cries (or whispers), 'I'm so confused – what can I do?' (1160). When Mencía suggests that he hide, he discloses, 'I never knew fear until now' (1163–5). He then loses his dagger behind Mencía's bed, the weapon soon to be found by Don Gutierre, and later to be presented to the King as evidence of Enrique's offense.

By the middle of Act Two, even the Prince's closest personal aide, Don Arias, refuses, at considerable risk, to assist him further in his dishonourable

---

13   See Ortiz Lottman on the potentially fatal harm that the loss of such a wager could inflict on Coquín.

scheme. Warned by King Pedro in Act Three to desist, and to respect a vassal's sphere, Enrique replies that he will continue the chase, and that with time he will be victorious – although his seemingly unshakable resolve is soon shaken. In the course of this heated conversation, Pedro demands that Enrique take the weapon. As Pedro presents the itinerant dagger to Enrique, the King's hand is cut. Pedro construes the event as an attempt at murder, and the Prince (for the second time) drops the dagger, choosing to go far away, 'so that you won't imagine of me that I could spill your blood. I'm so unhappy' (2280–2). Enrique, departing Seville in haste, sends Coquín to deliver to Mencía what turns out to be for her the definitively fatal lie: that she is the cause of his leaving.

Don Gutierre

As *The Physician of His Honour* opens, its protagonist, Don Gutierre Alfonso Solís, is enjoying a quiet rural life with his spouse Mencía. Finding that a royal party has descended on his home, Gutierre exhibits extreme deference toward Prince Enrique. So smitten is he with the royal presence that he leaves almost immediately for Seville to serve the King and the Prince, 'since I owe to his fall the honour that our house has won today' (509–11). In Act Two, Gutierre's growing suspicions of betrayal propel him into labyrinthine inner dialogues and bloody flights of fancy. Late in the act, he contemplates before his horrified wife what he would do were he to become jealous,

> of no more than a slave woman, or a maidservant, because of an imagined shadow – with inhuman force, I would rip out her heart in pieces with my own hands; and then, drenched in blood, unbound in fire, I would eat her heart by mouthfuls, I would drink her blood, I would rip out her soul, and if her soul were capable of pain, I swear to God! I would tear it to pieces. (2021–31)

Despite this consuming passion that threatens to overwhelm Gutierre, at some point between the end of Act Two and the beginning of Act Three he has composed himself and moved his household (counter-intuitively) into Seville, where his rival resides. In the face of apparent persistence against his honour by Enrique, he now appeals to the King to end the Prince's designs. But although the innocence of his wife is confirmed in Gutierre's hearing (see lines 2218–22 and 2916–22), matters go badly awry. When the dust settles and he is left alone, and once again in possession of Enrique's dagger, Gutierre declares, 'With a single act let us tear out the roots of so much evil.

Let Mencía die; ... and since today the Prince surrenders his dagger to me for the second time, ... let her die by it' (2303–5, 2307–9).

Doña Mencía

Mencía's is a totally domestic existence: all the scenes in which she appears take place in her home or her garden. Her trust and confidence in her attendant, the slave woman Jacinta, provide glimpses into Mencía's past and her emotional experiences. Mencía reveals that before her union with Gutierre, she had been wooed pleasurably by Prince Enrique – but apparently (see note to lines 289–92), because of her steadfastness and despite his persistence, within the strict bounds of honour. Evidently their social difference precluded marriage (302–6); and in Enrique's absence Mencía's father 'trampled on my freedom' (569–70) by marrying her to Don Gutierre. When, as the play begins, the Prince reappears in her life, she remains deeply concerned about his wellbeing, but also about her honour: 'once I had love', she tells Jacinta; 'now I have honour' (573).

Mencía is thus portrayed with a rich emotional life. Her spirit and quick wit – at least early in the play – are clear to the audience in her double-edged public conversation with Enrique, and her private verbal playfulness and sarcasm with Gutierre. But despite her resolve to protect her honour, Mencía extends to Enrique a thinly-veiled invitation to return to speak with 'the lady' (421). Although we learn that the Prince would have pursued Mencía regardless, she takes upon herself the full blame for his incriminating return to her home (1096). For the rest of the play Mencía tries to fend off the Prince. During his clandestine appearance early in Act Two she is resourceful, but once she spies a dagger in Gutierre's hand Mencía is overcome by fear and profound melancholy. From this point on, others control her actions. In panic she follows Jacinta's disastrous advice, and finally reacts to the prospect of impending death with dread but only feeble protest.

Doña Leonor

Throughout the play Doña Mencía's honour problems are interwoven with those of Doña Leonor. As *The Physician* opens, Leonor's honour has already been compromised by Don Gutierre. With apparently no male relatives to champion her, Leonor is assertive and outspoken – perhaps because it is her nature; perhaps also because she has nothing to lose in terms of honour. In Act One she persuades the King to take on her cause, asking Pedro to force Don Gutierre, who cannot now marry her, to bear the expense of her entering

Photos from the Brandeis Theater Company production of 'The Physician of His Honour', November 2006

The opening scene of the play: Don Arias (Joshua Davies), Prince Enrique (Kara Manson), and Don Diego (Eli Matzner)

Doña Mencia (Rebecca Webber) and Don Gutierre (Robert Serrell)

King Pedro (Anthony Mark Stockard)

Act 1: Doña Leonor (Lindsey McWhorter) with Don Diego, Don Pedro, and Don Arias

Doña Leonor

Prince Enrique

Jacinta (Allison Vanouse)   *Coquín (Matthew Crider)*

Cast and final setting

a convent. José Amezcua (pp. 261–70; p. 312) points out that unlike Mencía, who is trapped in the home, Leonor moves about and actively pursues her goal. Yet at the end she willingly exchanges her mobility for marriage to the only man capable of restoring her reputation, Gutierre the wife-murderer.

Leonor's tenacity and assertiveness contrast with Mencía's demeanor. Her pursuit of justice brings to light Gutierre's history of extravagant concern with honour, as well as his fondness for his wife, and underscores the King's interest in seeing justice done, regardless of the means of the petitioner. She is the catalyst for Don Arias's about-face in Act Two, as he stands up to his master Prince Enrique's dishonourable conduct. And Leonor is, finally, a partner in the marriage that superficially restores order at the end of the play.

Jacinta

Jacinta, a branded slave,[14] is Mencía's servant and confidante. A strong woman, her pursuit of freedom contributes to the destruction of her mistress. On the promise of emancipation, she paves the way for Enrique's surreptitious visit to her mistress, and assists in his escape when Gutierre returns unexpectedly. In the final act, when Coquín brings Don Enrique's

---

14 The play takes place in the fourteenth century when most slaves in Christian Spain were Muslims. Medieval Europe had ended enslavement of Christians by then (although infidels could not gain their freedom by converting to Christianity). By Calderón's time, Black African slaves were the most numerous and many were employed as household servants (see Kamen, pp. 109–10; Domínguez Ortiz pp. 162–5, p. 311; and Phillips pp. 107–13, pp. 160–70). According to Phillips (p. 162), 'African slaves in Seville, as in contemporary Portugal, enjoyed a considerably better reputation than Muslim or Morisco slaves, who were considered recalcitrant, hostile, and liable to run away'.

Covarrubias noted that 'runaway and disobedient' slaves were branded on the cheeks with what he believed to be an 'S' and 'I' (which looked like a nail), meaning '*sine iure* [without privilege]; because the slave is not his own but his master's, and therefore any free act is prohibited to him' (p. 491b). In Calderón's *The Mayor of Zalamea* (*El alcalde de Zalamea*), the protagonist Pedro Crespo offers himself and his son in slavery to Captain Alvaro, stating that the Captain could 'mark the two of us with an S and a nail today and sell us' (*poner una S y un clavo / hoy a los dos y vendernos*) (2276–7).

Since Jacinta is branded and Calderón makes no reference to her race or colour, it is likely that she is a Muslim or Morisca (a Muslim who has formally converted to Christianity). For the audience, therefore, the brands would signify that Jacinta is a slave, troublesome, probably Moorish or Morisca, and consequently untrustworthy and morally suspect. Moorish slave women as go-betweens in love affairs were familiar in contemporary writing. There is also evidence that Gutierre's servant Coquín may be of Moorish origins (see note 16 below).

message to Mencía, it is Jacinta who suggests that Mencía write the fatal letter to Enrique, and Jacinta who suggests the means by which the letter can be delivered.

Don Arias and Don Diego

Don Arias and Don Diego are the deferential personal aides (*privados* or 'royal favourites') of Prince Enrique and King Pedro, respectively. While their physical presence enhances the majesty projected by the two royal characters, their words at times undermine the authority of their masters. At the beginning of the play, both comment negatively about the King, and both appear to be involved in supporting the Prince's pursuit of Mencía.[15] Nevertheless, Arias later decides on moral grounds to refuse to participate in Enrique's designs. Diego also accompanies the King on one of his incognito night excursions about Seville, their conversations giving the audience one set of insights into the King's attitudes and concerns.

Coquín

Coquín is a member of Don Gutierre's household, and the master's personal attendant. His origins are opaque, his morality ambiguous, and his loyalties uncertain.[16] He plays the role of *gracioso* or *bufón* – which in the Golden Age

---

15   When Don Arias is arrested at the end of Act One, the Prince turns to Diego for help (1004–6).

16   'Coquín' is an unusual name, not appearing in any other work of early modern Spanish literature of which we are aware. For the contemporary audience it would conjure up a variety of associations relevant to the figure Calderón has created. 'Coquín' is a diminutive of *coco*, or coconut. Covarrubias (p. 325b) notes that the inner [brown] coconut has three holes 'that appear to be the eyes and mouth' and that Spaniards gave the name *coco* to the nut because they already used *coco* to refer to a facial expression that a monkey makes when annoyed and cries, 'Ko, ko'. For children, *coco* is 'a frightening figure, none more so than those that are dark or black in colour' (p. 326a) (see Randel, p. 878). According to *Autoridades* (I, p. 392c), *coco* also refers to 'a certain worm or species of moth that grows in or gets into seeds and fruits, and damages them in such a way that they are spoiled'. A variation of the word, possibly relevant, is *recoquín*, which Covarrubias defines as 'the very small and fat man' (p. 853a). In the dictionary of sixteenth-century French compiled by Huguet, among the meanings of *coquin* are: a beggar ('mendiant', II, p. 539b); one who is extremely poor ('celui qui est extremement pauvre', p. 540a); one who entreats obsequiously, a parasite ('solliciteur, parasite', p. 540b). In modern French the word means 'rascal' or 'rogue'. (With thanks to Michael Randall.)

Our information about Coquín's past is inconsistent. In Act One he reports to the King, 'I get into every house, although right now I eat my midday meal in the house of don Gutierre

comedia corresponds inexactly with the fool or court jester of Elizabethan theatre, and is a distant descendant of the chorus in classical Greek theatre. He is, then, a source of leavening humour, and his commentary illuminates the behaviour and character of his superiors.

But Coquín is also crucial to the plot. As a messenger, he both incites the tragedy and tries to avert it. Although he is Gutierre's servant, in Act Three he brings the fateful message from Prince Enrique to Mencía, dupes her into hearing it (2362–9), and then agrees to Jacinta's suggestion that he bear the reply. Yet this opportunist at last chooses to carry out 'an honourable action, by a man who is, after all is said and done, well born' (2728–9). Coquín approaches the King on the streets of Seville in a futile attempt to save Mencía (and in so doing, once more betrays his master). Coquín's final act in the play is to identify for Pedro and entourage the house of Don Gutierre, where the scene of horror is revealed.

THE METAPHOR

The central metaphor of the play is expressed in the title. Don Gutierre is the physician, and his honour the sick patient; Don Gutierre diagnoses his honour's malady, and reflects on how to cure it. His ruminations are not always rational, nor is his poetic imagery always consistent, but a striking cure *is* presented.

In fact, medical language makes its entrance in the opening scene of *The Physician*, when Enrique's accident seems to put his life in mortal danger, and Don Arias speaks of 'seek[ing] a remedy for him' (119). It is Mencía who first dons the metaphorical mantle of 'physician' when early in Act Two she determines 'to cure this disease before it strikes' (1243), and proceeds to devise a subterfuge explaining the presence of a strange man in the house. Soon thereafter, Gutierre's discovery of a dagger behind Mencía's bed marks

---

Alfonso …' (749–53). But in the third act Gutierre says to Coquín, 'you've always served me nobly; you were raised in my home…' (2443–4). One may speculate, as in Jacinta's case (see note 15 above), that Coquín is of Moorish origins. In Act One, he exclaims to the King, 'Praise Allah!' (705). An ambiguous statement, also made to Pedro (754), may have Coquín hailing from Córdoba, one of the last Muslim strongholds in Spain. He refers to himself as 'a man who is, after all is said and done, well born' (2728–30) – although he is now obviously of lowly status in Christian Spain. The brown colour of the inner coconut may imply a dark complexion; and Coquín's readiness to desert Gutierre when imprisonment looms, and then to betray both master and mistress, would be to the Spanish Christian audience unsurprising behaviour for a man of his background.

the moment when his suspicions of betrayal are aroused, and it is when he matches the dagger to Enrique's sword that Gutierre first calls himself 'the physician of his honour' (1673). Intending 'to stop the sickness in its tracks' (1671), speaking both to himself and of himself as the doctor, he prescribes

> first, a diet of silence: hold your tongue and be patient. Next, he says that you should apply to your wife sweet words, pleasantries, pleasures, love, flattery: these are defensive forces, so that the illness won't worsen due to neglect. Because with women, and especially with one's wife, emotional scenes, arguments, jealousy, criticism, and suspicions sicken more than they cure. (1674–86)

Despite his determination at this point 'to see how advanced the malady is' (1689–90), within twenty lines Gutierre raises the prospect of 'the final cure' (1711). That night, as he visits his 'sick [male] patient' (*mi enfermo*, 1874), Mencía in the dark mistakenly addresses him as 'Your Highness' (1931). Gutierre speaks to himself of 'revenge' (1948) and 'kill[ing] her' (1977), ending the act with the ominous decision: 'Since I call myself the physician of my honour, I'll bury my dishonour in the ground' (2047–8). While it seems clear at this point that the physician has made his diagnosis and decided on the course of treatment, at the beginning of the next act he speaks to the King of 'curing' his honour 'with prevention' (2090–2). He describes the preventive measures he has taken:

> I didn't act jealous with my wife, and since then I've been even more loving. I used to live in a charming and peaceful country home; but to keep her from being sad in that solitude, I moved my household to Seville, where she has everything she could possibly desire. Abuse is for despicable husbands, who grow accustomed to their grievances when they put them into words. (2145–58)

Nevertheless, Gutierre eventually does proceed with 'the final cure' (2478), which brings his honour back to health, the site of the malady – Mencía – having been eliminated.

Afterwards he makes a false report to the King and companions, in which Mencía becomes the ailing patient, and 'a very illustrious physician, a man of the greatest reputation' (2836–9) prescribes a remedy, which fails due to 'a grievous mortal accident' (2832). But in the end, for Leonor as well as for the King, Gutierre casts aside the pretense of Mencía's illness and the renowned physician's failed cure. Consenting to give his hand to

Leonor, he warns her 'that it comes bathed in blood' (2943–4), and 'that I've been the physician of my honour, and my science is not forgotten' (2946–8). Leonor's response reveals a confusion or conflation of his false report with his metaphor, as she invites her new husband to apply his science to her: 'Cure me with it, should I become ill' (2948–9).[17]

HISTORICAL CONTEXTS AND RESPONSES

Marriage is a classic ending of comedy,[18] because it signals a 'happy ending', the restoration of order. However, the marriage arranged at the conclusion of *The Physician of His Honour* has caused a great deal of disorder among readers and spectators over the years, since it follows quickly on the prospective husband's annihilation of his first wife. Rather than questioning Calderón's uses or subversions of literary conventions, generations of readers and playgoers instead questioned his morals. Hispanists were offended by the display of immorality at the conclusion of this and the other two honour plays by Calderón, believing that the judgment of the rulers overseeing the dénouements reflected Calderón's own point of view.[19] *The Physician of His Honour*, like *The Painter of His Dishonour* and *Secret Wrong, Secret Revenge*, helped create a perception of this writer as a brutal man, an advocate of wife-murder for imagined offenses. In Spain, the adjective 'Calderonian' (*calderoniano*) became pejorative, used to describe obsessively jealous and punctilious husbands, or tales of violent spousal revenge.

More recently, academics began to rehabilitate Calderón and his *comedias*. Taking into account the contexts of the two 'wife-murder' plays embedded in

---

17 Wardropper (1958) was the first to call attention to the importance in the play of the central medical conceit. He pointed out that most previous scholarly treatment of *The Physician*, in addition to condemning the *comedia* on moral grounds, judged the work too harshly because it did not measure up to nineteenth-century standards of realism. *The Physician*, Wardropper observed, is dramatic poetry, and at times the poetic conceit prevails over logic. Thus Gutierre's actions during the play, though not always explicable in rational terms, make sense poetically: he calls himself a physician and his decisions are guided by conformity to this medical metaphor. We would point out, however, that Gutierre invokes the imagery inconsistently, and manipulates it according to the circumstances in which he finds himself. Gutierre governs the metaphor, rather than the reverse.

18 That is, 'comedy' in general, as opposed to the Golden Age *comedia*.

19 In an essay first published in 1881, the influential Marcelino Menéndez y Pelayo called Calderón's honour dramas 'radically immoral' (p. 229), while still noting that they provide a good warning to wives not to stray (p. 233).

historical circumstances – *The Physician* and *Secret Wrong* – permitted ironic readings of their conclusions.[20] In the case of *The Physician*, scholars identified a major historical tradition that stamped King Pedro of Castile (r. 1350–69) with the sobriquet 'the Cruel' (*el Cruel*). Now horror and revulsion were considered the proper and intended reaction to Pedro's actions in the dénouement of this drama, and Gutierre became cruel by virtue of his close association with the King. The revised view made it possible to reconcile the devoutly Christian Calderón so admired by Goethe (see Sullivan, pp. 185–95) with the Calderón that created these dramas of uxoricide.[21]

It is worth noting, however, that *The Physician of His Honour*, like any literary classic, continues to be contested and redefined by succeeding generations and varying schools of interpretation. Further investigation of written and oral traditions, including chronicles and ballads, has influenced evaluations of the royal characters, and so of Calderón. It was learned that Pedro had in fact become the subject of different historical reputations that were at odds with one another: by his detractors he was known as a cruel and sexually aberrant tyrant (see Weissberger, p. 81); by his partisans as a strict enforcer of justice and a champion of the common people against the nobility.

In fact, *The Physician*'s two royal characters, King Pedro of Castile and his bastard half-brother Enrique, were widely known in the seventeenth century for their turbulent and at last deadly relationship in the fourteenth century. Supported by the aristocracy, the Prince faced off in civil war against the King, and eventually murdered him with a dagger. As King Enrique II (r. 1369–79) – a progenitor of the royal houses of both Aragon and Castile, and of both King Ferdinand and Queen Isabella – he was able to ensure that accounts written during his reign depicted himself as a hero and his dead half-brother as a tyrant (see Gimeno Casalduero, pp. 81–91). Nearly all subsequent written histories accepted and perpetuated this portrayal. Juan de Mariana, the eminent Jesuit historian, writes in 1601 of King Pedro's 'bloody and terrible disposition'.[22] According to Mariana, the monarch committed many vengeful, treacherous, and extremely cruel acts. 'King Pedro did not consider how abhorrent and hateful he was becoming, and what people would say about him not just then, but also in the centuries to come' (p. 101).

---

20   And by association, of Calderón's third, non-historical *drama de honor*, *The Painter of His Dishonour*.

21   See the ground-breaking articles of E. M. Wilson, 'Gerald Brenan's Calderón', and Alexander A. Parker, 'Towards a Definition of Calderonian Tragedy'.

22   P. 92. Page references are to the Spanish edition of Mariana.

However, two conflicting oral traditions existed. Many ballads originating during the civil war survived until – and were published in – Calderón's day. While some ballads favour Prince Enrique, others take King Pedro's side. And seventeenth-century dramatists found the King's a rich character to exploit, evoking one or the other – sometimes both – of his opposing personae, which were summed up in the epithets 'the Cruel' (*el Cruel*) and 'the Enforcer of Justice' (*el Justiciero*).[23] Some plays, for example Lope de Vega's *The Royal Audiences of King Pedro* (*Audiencias del Rey don Pedro*) and *Here Comes the Girl from Mazagatos* (*Ya anda la de Mazagatos*), hold him up as an exemplary leader, whereas *The Ramírez de Arellano Family* (*Los Ramírez de Arellano*), also by Lope, is highly critical.[24] Juan Ruiz de Alarcón's *Winning Friends* (*Ganar amigos*), which includes 'King Pedro, Enforcer of Justice' ('*el Rey don Pedro el Justiciero*'), portrays the monarch learning to temper justice with mercy.

Therefore, literary critics have found themselves with traditions that support a wide range of interpretations of Calderón's *The Physician of His Honour*, King Pedro's character being the focus of the most intense debate. Whether he deserves to be considered cruel or just, both or neither, has preoccupied a number of investigators.[25]

The large body of scholarship on *The Physician* continues to grow,

---

23   The phrase 'el Justiciero' poses a problem for translators, since there is no expression that corresponds exactly in English. In the Spanish of the period it implies one who is strict and even cruel in seeing to the enforcement of justice. Covarrubias defines 'justiciero' as 'he who upholds the rigor of justice; he must have a little cruelty in him, because *summum ius, summa iniuria* – the extremity of the law is the extremity of injustice' (p. 692b). A century later the *Diccionario de Autoridades* defines 'justiciero' as 'one who observes justice exactly. It is often used for one who punishes crimes with some severity' (II, p. 337a). Obviously, 'el Cruel' and 'el Justiciero' are not mutually exclusive, but in the traditions related to King Pedro, one is clearly pejorative, and the other is used in a positive sense.

Scholars seeking an English equivalent for 'el Justiciero' have opted either for 'the Just' or 'the Justicer'. 'The Just' carries no real suggestion of severity, nor does 'the Justicer' which, besides being an archaic term that would be unfamiliar to modern readers or playgoers, means 'one who maintains or executes justice; a supporter or vindicator of right' (*Oxford English Dictionary*). We have settled on 'the Enforcer of Justice' as more nearly conveying the sense of 'justiciero' in Calderón's time.

24   See Exum on the evolution of portrayals of King Pedro, from positive to negative, across eight of Lope's plays featuring the monarch as a character.

25   For example, while Parker (1957, pp. 3–4) finds Calderón's Pedro cruel, Watson maintains that the character is just, and Cruickshank (1970) believes the King bungles his genuine efforts to achieve justice.

with historical, psychological, feminist, and other approaches. A useful and concise starting-point for the student or scholar wishing to delve deeper into commentary on this fascinating play is Don Cruickshank's 2003 critical guide for the Grant & Cutler series, which includes an annotated bibliography. Among studies of note, in 1982 Cruickshank himself suggests that certain references to blood and the ritual nature of Gutierre's utterances recall pseudo-Jewish ritual, which would help condemn him in the eyes of an early modern Spanish audience.[26] Benabu (1982) notes parallels between the protagonist's actions and King Pedro's reputation in some ballads and historical accounts as a wife-murderer (see Cruz 1992). Soufas analyzes the characters in terms of seventeenth-century theories of psychology, with emphasis on imbalances in the four humours. El Saffar, McKendrick (1992), Cruz (2001), and Dopico Black, among others, have discussed the play in light of issues relating to gender.

STAGING AND SETTING

In seventeenth-century Madrid there were two public theatres, or *corrales*, both of them open to the elements and originally improvised from a space enclosed by buildings. Public seating was segregated by gender, while more affluent playgoers could engage private rooms in the surrounding buildings overlooking the performance. Members of the clergy were seated in the attics of these buildings. Also available was standing room in front of the stage, which was occupied by those who could afford only the cheapest admission – at prices so low that the *comedia* reached a wide range of social classes.[27] Performances took place in the afternoon with little or no artificial lighting.[28]

At the Corral del Príncipe in Madrid (site of the Teatro Español today), actors performed on an apron stage rising six feet above the ground. There was very little scenery, which meant that the audience was called upon largely to imagine the setting, based on cues from the dialogue, actions on the stage, and costuming. For example, much of *The Physician* takes place at night, with 'extinguishing' (or 'killing') the light an important motif.

---

26   Spain had expelled the Jews in 1492, and suspicion followed those who converted to Christianity, as well as their descendants.

27   On the economics of the *comedia* and the social makeup of the playgoing public, see Greer and Junguito.

28   On staging of the *comedia*, see Shergold (1967, pp. 383–414, p. 552), Allen (1983), Ruano de la Haza (1988), Ruano de la Haza and Allen (1994).

Spectators had to imagine these conditions in broad daylight. Curtains normally hung across the back of the stage, perhaps concealing left and right exits as well as at the center what is known as a discovery space. Patricia Kenworthy speculates that characters in *The Physician* who hide – such as Leonor at the King's instruction in Act One – would normally have looked out from behind one of the curtains – or a piece of scenery – so that they remained partially visible to the audience.[29] The central curtain would have been drawn open on three occasions in *The Physician*: when Don Gutierre arrives at the country home late in Act Two and moves it to discover Mencía asleep; when he arrives at the Seville home in Act Three to discover his wife writing to the Prince; and when near the end of the play he 'discovers' Mencía's corpse to the King and his companions.[30]

TRANSLATING AND EDITING CALDERÓN

Many intermediaries – among them, editors, teachers, directors, actors – influence the way readers or spectators experience a play. In the case of the translator, even if a conscious decision is taken to refrain from advocating for any single understanding of the work, differences in culture; geography; and the passage of centuries, among other variables, inevitably influence the words chosen; and these words contain an attitude toward the events. Translation necessarily produces a personal imprint on whatever text is chosen to represent the original.

---

29 She points out that an exception would be in Act Two when Gutierre arrives home unexpectedly and Enrique hides in Mencía's bedroom, 'behind that canopy' (1161). Kenworthy writes, 'If the audience is to believe (with any sort of realism) that Enrique has entered the house, hidden behind the bed and dropped his dagger, then he can't remain in view of the audience *al paño* (at the curtain)' (Patricia Kenworthy, personal communication of August 9, 1995).

30 McKendrick comments on the dramatic impact of the first and third discoveries: 'This sudden vision (in Act Two] of the innocent, beautiful wife in the confined inner stage deep in a sleep that counterfeits death is a vivid prefiguration of the final, obscene revelation of her lifeless body on the blood-soaked bed; it adds enormous weight to the play's repeated depiction of Mencía as a confined and passive figure and of Gutierre as an active, predatory one' (1992, p. 237).

Kenworthy has suggested to us the possibility of an earlier discovery involving the central curtain, which would anticipate the three later movements by Gutierre. Near the beginning of the second act, the Prince may open the curtain as he comes upon Mencía where she sleeps. See also Benabu 1991; Fischer; and Cruickshank 2003, pp. 25–34.

That said, in both editions of *The Physician of His Honour*, the translators have made certain judgments and chosen specific wording based on knowledge of the original and the second language as well as cultural contexts. Documented information about the play's fourteenth-century historical setting available to Calderón and his audience (including written and oral traditions), and about the playwright's seventeenth-century historical context (including biography, conventions of the genre, staging, early modern Spanish, and other elements of the cultural milieu), inform the translation.

The process of reading itself produces an interpretation, and it is hoped that this version of *The Physician of His Honour* will furnish the reader a coherent basis for her or his own 'production' of the play.

Language and Style

Calderón is a masterful and highly controlled writer. Clearly, the drama has been carefully planned and reworked, in its construction as a whole (see 'Structure', above) and in its articulation. Certain words, phrases, and motifs (for example, variations on *confusión, turbar* [to disturb], *matar la luz* [killing or extinguishing the light], and of course, the medical imagery) are repeated at strategic points throughout the play, corroborating Wardropper's characterization (1958) of *The Physician of His Honour* as a well wrought dramatic poem.

Specific words recur in the text to set the basic broad theme of the play – most obviously *honor, honra* (honour), *agravio* (offense), and, for Gutierre's particular experience of honour, *celos* (jealousy). Some 'mood' words are used widely but more especially in the final act: *desdicha* (misfortune), *triste/tristeza* (sad/sadness), and *enojos* (tribulation). The translator must decide whether to repeat the English vocabulary when the poet repeats these and other key words. There are times when the reiteration of the word calls attention to links among characters and situations. For example, in Act Three, Gutierre overhears the highly charged conversation between the King and the Prince that results in Pedro's wound and Enrique's decision to leave Seville. Gutierre's soliloquy, in which he declares twice, 'Let Mencía die' (2305; 2315), is followed by a clearing of the stage and change of scene. Next we are presented with an exchange between Mencía and Jacinta. The final line of Gutierre's speech concludes as he describes himself as *triste* (sad); the next line spoken, by Jacinta, describes Mencía's *tristeza* (sadness):

GUTIERRE	¿No hay, claros cielos, decidme,
	para un desdichado muerte?
	¿No hay un rayo para un triste?
	(2326–8)
JACINTA	Señora, ¿qué tristeza
	turba la admiración a tu belleza,
	que la noche y el día
	no haces sino llorar? (2329–32)
GUTIERRE	Clear blue skies, tell me, why don't
	you cast down a lightning bolt to
	strike me dead? How can you not
	take pity on a man as sad as I?
JACINTA	Madam, what sadness plagues
	you? Day and night you do nothing
	but weep.

However, there are times during the play when the same Spanish word in a new context gains a nuance not conveyed in the English used earlier, or when a different English word will impart a 'correct' meaning and sound better, too – admittedly, at some cost to Calderón's consistency in poetic diction, but cost is inevitable when translating from one language to another. Had a verse translation been undertaken, factoring rhythm and rhyme into word choice, the loss would have been greater, although the sense of the play as a dramatic poem might have been enhanced.

An instance of departure from Calderón's regular lexicon can be found in this edition's diverse translations of one recurring word, *confusión*. Seldom occurring in the Spanish of the first two acts, it is much used and important in the third, emphasizing the tangle of mistaken perceptions and the dark mood leading to the finale. The English varies with the situations. For example:

- Prince Enrique, having cut the hand of his brother the King, cries out, '¿Hay confusiones más tristes?' (Can there be a sadder misunderstanding than this?) (2276)
- Mencía ponders the possibility that 'En una confusión de confusiones' ([in] one crazy, immeasurable confusion out of many) in the dark she may have disastrously mistaken Gutierre for the Prince (2334).
- Ludovico asks Gutierre, '¿Qué confusiones son éstas, / que a tal extremo me traen?' (What bewildering events are these, that bring me to such a pass? (2566–7).

- And the King charges that shadowy figures in the darkened streets play tricks 'a darme / confusión' (to confound me) (2659–60).

Once the King has been informed of the likely wife murder, *confusión* exits the stage. At no time does Gutierre, in public or in private, admit to being 'confused' – he is, after all, a self-proclaimed man of science.

Attempting faithfully to translate Calderón's style is a great challenge, particularly with certain characters in certain situations. In some of the descriptive or contemplative speeches, his complex technique is indebted to the baroque manner of the poet Luis de Góngora (1561–1627). Mencía's report to Jacinta of the Prince's accident is characteristic of a type of passage in Calderón recalling Góngora's exquisite creation and manipulation of imagery. An opening question, thesis statement, or reference to an event ('something terrible has happened' [48–9]) is followed by elaboration in vivid similes and metaphors. Concluding the passage will be a virtuoso summation of all the previous elements introduced.

> A gallant knight came on a steed so swift that it seemed like a bird flying in the wind, painting the air with a crest of plumes. The splendours of the field and of the sun competed with each other in those plumes: the field sent flowers, and the sun sent stars, because the crest bloomed and shone. One moment it was the sun, and the next, it was a spring meadow. When the galloping horse stumbled, the bird fell to the earth and became a rose. And so in its brilliance the crest simulated the sun, sky, earth, and wind; bird, brute, star and flower. (49–72)

This diction is not intended to be realistic. It fixes attention on the speaker as her lyrical narration accumulates and reaches its climax in the concluding register of images[31]. In addition to this speech by Mencía, similarly crafted contemplations of themes appear in passages spoken by Prince Enrique, Doña Leonor, and especially by Don Gutierre: first, in his obsequious addresses to the Prince; and later in his tormented soliloquies.

Also representative of Calderón's poetry – and common in Renaissance and Baroque expression throughout Europe – are references to classical literature and mythology, which lend an air of timelessness and grandeur (and occasionally of hyperbole) to the language. Prince Enrique is associated in *The Physician* both with Actaeon, the hunter who was to be turned into

---

31   See Dámaso Alonso, '*La correlación en la estructura del teatro calderoniano*'.

a stag and torn apart by his own hounds (1049–50);[32] and (contradictorily) Aeneas, the heroic Trojan prince who eventually founded Rome.[33] At the beginning of Act Three, Gutierre calls King Pedro 'Spanish Apollo, ... Castilian Atlas, whose shoulders carry an entire orb, a planet of sapphire, a globe of diamond, constant and enduring ...' (2053–8). He then assures the King that in virtue Mencía is 'far more honest, chaste, and steadfast even than Lucretia, Portia, and Tomyris' (2121–2).

The speech of certain characters is particularly distinctive. Coquín's language is marked by topical references, puns, and witty variations on themes that also require explanatory footnotes when they resist literal translation into English. An example is his manipulation of 'compás de pies' (two-footed compass; see lines 726–8 note) in Act One. And then there is King Pedro, a man of few words – which reinforces other characters' judgments of him as either cruel or a strict enforcer of justice. His sentences tend to be brief and blunt, often enigmatic in their elliptical quality. When near the end of the play Gutierre reveals Mencía's body (2871+), the King declares, 'A remarkable subject!' (¡Notable sujeto! [2872]). This reaction could be taken in a number of different ways. Is he horrified, does he endorse what he sees, or both? And what (or who) is the 'subject' to which he refers?[34]

Still, it is inevitable that some references in *The Physician* that would have been current in different sectors of the seventeenth-century Spanish public will today be lost to us. We must be content with scouring extant resources such as dictionaries, chronicles, emblem collections, other literary works, and the Spanish language of today for clues to meaning.

Versification

In *The New Art of Writing Plays*, Lope de Vega stresses the importance of choosing different types of poetry for different situations in the *comedia*.

> acomode los versos con prudencia
> a los sujetos de que va tratando;
> las décimas son buenas para quejas,
> el soneto está bien en los que aguardan,
> las relaciones piden los romances

---

32 On implications of the the Actaeon imagery, see Fox 2001.
33 See lines 131 and 240–2, and the accompanying notes. For speculation on the contradictory imagery associated with Prince Enrique, see Fox 1996.
34 See line 2872 note.

> aunque en octavas lucen por extremo,
> son los tercetos para cosas graves,
> y para las de amor las redondillas .... (p. 162)

Tactfully suit your verse to the subjects being treated. *Décimas* are good for complainings; the sonnet is good for those who are waiting in expectation; recitals of events ask for *romances*, though they shine brilliantly in *octavas*. Tercets are for grave affairs and *redondillas* for affairs of love.... (pp. 34–5)

Over the years, scholars have studied verse patterns for evidence of authorship and date of composition as well as to appreciate better the tone contributed to scenes and situations by the verse employed. Following is a synopsis of the versification in *The Physician*, with thanks to Cruickshank (1989). For a discussion of Spanish verse forms, see 'Versification' in Martel, Alpern, and Mades.

Act I: lines	1–76	redondilla
	77–314	romance é–o (153–4, estribillo)
	315–574	décima
	575–608	silva
	609–72	octava
	673–1020	romance é
Act II: lines	1021–42	romance ú–e
	1143–70	redondilla
	1171–1402	décima (1381–1392, décima irregular)
	1403–74	romance á–e
	1475–84	décima
	1485–1524	romance á–e
	1525–84	décima
	1585–1712	romance é–a (1609–10, 1657–8, 1711–2 estribillo)
	1713–1860	redondilla
	1861–2048	silva
Act III: lines	2049–2108	décima
	2109–2328	romance í–e
	2329–2507	silva
	2508–2725	romance á–e
	2726–2813	redondilla
	2814–2953	romance á–a

THE EDITION

The starting point for Calderón's Spanish in this volume is the second edition of *El médico de su honra* prepared by Don W. Cruickshank for Castalia in 1989, which is grounded in editions printed mostly during Calderón's lifetime.[35] Occasionally we diverge from Cruickshank in matters of punctuation and staging. Our notes to the English and Spanish texts sometimes refer to Cruickshank's notes, as well as to earlier editions of *El médico de su honra* by C. A. Jones, Bruce W. Wardropper, and Ángel Valbuena Briones; and to other relevant texts and scholarship. Brackets indicate stage directions not present in the earliest editions. Italicized asterisks within brackets, '*[* * *]*', designate a clearing of the stage and change of location.

Some notes to *The Physician/El médico* are intended to answer technical questions both the native Spanish speaker and the student of Spanish might ask about the original language; for example, on the use of the future subjunctive 'oyere' (277); or contractions and archaisms such as 'desta' (30) and 'agora' (170). Most comments in the notes on subtleties of word choice can serve readers of the Spanish or of the English. An early example is the note on the subject of 'viniera' (7) in the opening lines of the play: it is ambiguous whether King Pedro laments coming to Seville himself, or that his brother has come.

Other notes supplement the English, sorting out double or even triple meanings; or bring in cultural and/or historical contexts, and comment on staging.

A WORD ON THE SECOND EDITION

As of this writing, a decade has passed since the first Aris & Phillips critical edition and translation of Calderón's *El médico de su honra* appeared. Donald Hindley and I collaborated on that volume, and this writer is responsible for the second edition. While the format and some of the critical apparatus remain essentially the same, the translation itself has undergone an extensive revision.

Since its first publication, classroom use of the volume showed that faithful rendering into English of complexities in Calderón's poetic diction

---

35 These are designated as QC (1637), S (1641), Q (1670), and VT (1686). See Cruickshank (1989, pp. 61–2) for detailed information about these early editions.

and sentence structure could prove distracting to readers. A poet sometimes uses hyperbaton, and repeats words that in the original language intensify meaning and enhance sound, whereas in English prose they may detract from clarity, especially when those words are spoken aloud. A principal aim of the new version is to simplify the English, while continuing to respect and acknowledge as much as possible the beauties and challenges of the original Spanish. Now, English word order is more natural; longer sentences are often shortened; and sometimes words that become superfluous in translation are eliminated. An example is late in Act Two, as Gutierre speaks with Mencía about the deadly wind that has extinguished the light. When he adds that she could very well lose her life to it, too (1999–2000), she replies, 'Entenderte pretendo/y aunque más lo procure, no te entiendo' (2001–02). While the first edition's translation is literal ('I'm trying to understand you, and no matter how hard I try, I don't understand'), in the second she simply states, 'I don't understand'.

The second edition remains a resource for consultation by the Spanish-reader and for the Spanish-language instructor wishing to discuss linguistic points. To this end, some of the complexities of the first version move into the notes to the second edition. For instance, in Act Three when King Pedro hides Gutierre behind the curtain, instructing him to keep silent no matter what he may hear, Gutierre answers, 'Seré el pájaro que fingen / con una piedra en la boca' (2178–79). The first edition reads, 'I'll be the bird that they describe with a stone in its mouth', with a footnote explaining the image. In the second version, the English is, 'My lips are sealed', and the more literal translation shifts to the footnote with the explanatory material.

Wayland, Massachusetts, May 2007

ACKNOWLEDGEMENTS

Parts of this revised Introduction are based on Fox, 'Some Thoughts on Editing, Translating, and Teaching *El médico de su honra*', in the *Bulletin of the Comediantes*.

I am grateful to the students in classes at Brandeis University who over the years let me know which passages of the first edition of the translation worked well, and which needed re-thinking. Mónica Viñao's and Eric Hill's 2006 production of the new version, performed by the Brandeis Theater company, brilliantly honoured Calderóns's creation. My thanks go to Scott Edmiston and David Colfer for making available photos from the production for use in this volume, and to Brandeis for helping underwrite the aquisition of the cover art. Kendra Harrison's sharp and knowledgeable eye as a proofreader has been indispensable. I would like to thank Don W. Cruickshank for again allowing the use of his critical edition of the play as a basis for the Spanish text; and Donald Hindley for his collaboration on the first editon of the translation. Finally, for putting up with very early mornings while this edition came into being, I blow a kiss to Katie Hindley.

BIBLIOGRAPHY

Allen, John J. *The Reconstruction of a Spanish Golden Age Playhouse: El Corral del Príncipe*. Gainesville 1983.

Alonso, Dámaso. 'La correlación en la estructura del teatro calderoniano'. In Dámaso Alonso and Carlos Bousoño. *Seis calas en la expresión literaria española*. Madrid 1951, 115–86.

Amezcua, José. *Lectura ideológica de Calderón: 'El médico de su honra'*. México, D.F. 1991.

Benabu, Isaac. 'Further Thoughts on King Pedro's Predicament at the End of Calderón's *El médico de su honra*'. *Bulletin of Hispanic Studies* 59 (1982): 26–32.

Benabu, Isaac. 'Interpreting the *Comedia* in the Absence of a Performance Tradition: Gutierre in Calderón's *El médico de su honra*'. In *Prologue to Performance: Spanish Classical Theatre Today*. (ed.) Louise and Peter Fothergill-Payne, Lewisburg, Pennsylvania 1991, 23–35.

Blue, William R. ' "¿Qué es esto que miro?": Converging Sign Systems in *El médico de su honra*'. *Bulletin of the Comediantes*, 30 (1978): 83–96.

Calderón de la Barca, Pedro. *El alcalde de Zalamea*. (ed.) Angel Valbuena Briones. Madrid 1984.

Calderón de la Barca, Pedro. *Love Is No Laughing Matter/No hay burlas con el amor*. (ed.) and Trans. Don W. Cruickshank and Seán Page. Warminster 1986.

Calderón de la Barca, Pedro. *El médico de su honra*. (ed.) Don W. Cruickshank. 2nd ed. Madrid 1989.

Casa, Frank P. 'Aspects of Characterization in Golden Age Drama'. In *Studies in Honor of Everett W. Hesse*. (ed.) William C. McCrary and José A. Madrigal. Lincoln, Nebraska 1981, 37–48.

Castro, Américo. *De la edad conflictiva*. Madrid 1961. Vol. I.

Corominas, Joan. *Diccionario crítico etimológico de la lengua castellana*. Bern 1970.

Correas, Gonzalo. *Vocabulario de refranes y frases proverbiales* [1627]. (ed.) Louis Combet. Rev. Robert Jammes and Maïté Mir-Andreu. Madrid 2000.

Covarrubias Orozco, Sebastián de. *Tesoro de la lengua castellana o española* [1611]. (ed.) Felipe C.R. Maldonado. Rev. Manuel Camarero. Madrid 1994.

Cruickshank, Don W. *Calderón de la Barca. El médico de su honra*. London 2003.

Cruickshank, Don W. 'Calderón's King Pedro: Just or Unjust?' *Spanische Forschungen* 25 (1970): 113–32.

Cruickshank, Don W. 'The Metaphorical *Criptojudaísmo* of Calderón's Gutierre'. *Bulletin of Hispanic Studies* 59 (1982): 26–41.

Cruickshank, Don W. and Seán Page. Introduction to *Love is no Laughing Matter* (*No hay burlas con el amor*) by Pedro Calderón de la Barca. Warminster 1986, vii–xxvii.

Cruz, Anne J. 'Eunuchs and Empty Houses: Coquín's Tragic Joke in *El médico de su honra*'. *Bulletin of the Comediantes* 53 (2001): 217–35.

Cruz, Anne J. 'The Politics of Illicit Love in the "Pedro el cruel" Ballad Cycle'. *Nordic Yearbook of Folklore* (1992 / 48): 1–16.

Cull, John. 'Emblematics in Calderón's *El médico de su honra*'. *Bulletin of the Comediantes* 44 (1992): 113–31.

Diccionario de Autoridades. Madrid 1979 [1724].

Dixon, Victor. (ed.) *El perro del hortelano* by Lope de Vega. London 1981.

Domínguez Ortiz, Antonio. *The Golden Age of Spain, 1516–1659*. New York 1971.

Dopico Black, Georgina. *Perfect Wives, Other Women: Adultery and Inquisition in Early Modern Spain*. Durham, North Carolina 2001.

El Saffar, Ruth. 'Anxiety of Identity: Gutierre's Case in El *médico de su honra*'. In *Studies in Honor of Bruce W. Wardropper*. (eds) Dian Fox, Harry Sieber, and Robert ter Horst. Newark, New Jersey 1989: 105–24.

Exum, Frances. *The Metamorphosis of Lope de Vega's King Pedro (The Treatment of Pedro I de Castilla in the Drama of Lope de Vega)*. Madrid 1974.

Fischer, Susan L. '*El médico de su honra*, Semiotics, and Performance: "An Exercise in Self-Exorcism"?' *Gestos: Teoría y Practica del Teatro Hispánico*, 15 (1993): 41–64.

Fox, Dian. 'The Literary Use of History: *El médico de su honra* in Contexts'. In '*El arte nuevo de estudiar comedias*': *Literary Theory and Golden Age Spanish Drama*. (ed.) Barbara Simerka. Lewisburg, Pennsylvania, 1996: 206–32. Rpt. rev. from *Kings in Calderón: A Study in Characterization and Political Theory*. London 1986: 67–84.

Fox, Dian. '"¡Notable sujeto!" Terms of Dismemberment in *El médico de su honra*'. *Bulletin of the Comediantes* 53 (2001): 197–216.

Fox, Dian. 'Some Thoughts on Editing, Translating, and Teaching *El médico de su honra*'. *Bulletin of the Comediantes* 58 (2006) [2007]: 421–33.

Gimeno Casalduero, Joaquín. *La imagen del monarca en la Castilla del siglo XIV: Pedro el Cruel, Enrique II y Juan I*. Madrid 1972.

Green, Otis H. *Spain and the Western Tradition: The Castilian Mind in Literature from 'El Cid' to Calderón*. Madison, Wisconsin 1968. 4 vols.

Greer, Margaret and Andrea Junguito. 'Economies of the Early Modern Spanish Stage'. In *Angulos y perspectivas. Reconsideraciones de la dramaturgia aurisecular*. (eds) Ignacio Arellano, Jesús Pérez-Magallones, and Juan Luis Suárez. *Revista Canadiense de Estudios Hispánicos* 29 (2004): 30–46.

Horace. *The Art of Poetry (Ars poetica)*. In *The Complete Works of Horace (Quintus Horatius Flaccus)*. (ed.) Charles E. Passage. New York 1983: 341–77.

Huguet, Edmond. *Dictionnaire de la langue française du seizième siècle*. Paris 1925–1967. 4 vols.

Jones, C.A., ed. *El médico de su honra*. By Pedro Calderón de la Barca. Oxford 1961.

Kamen, Henry. *Spain 1469–1714: A Society of Conflict*. New York 1983.

Larson, Donald. *The Honor Plays of Lope de Vega*. Cambridge, Massachusetts 1977.

McKendrick, Melveena. 'Gender and Symbolic Space in the Theatre of Calderon'. *Journal of the Institute of Romance Studies* I (1992): 225–38.

McKendrick, Melveena. *Woman and Society in the Spanish Drama of the Golden Age: A Study of the 'Mujer Varonil'*. London 1974.

Mariana, Juan de. *Historia general de España. Compuesto primero en latín, después buelta en castellano por Iuan de Mariana, doctor Theologo, de la Compañía de Iesus*. Vol. II. Toledo, 1601. Also available in *Obras del Padre Juan de Mariana*. (ed.) D.F. P[i] y M[argall]. Biblioteca de Autores Españoles, Vols. XXX–XXXI.

Martel, José and Hymen Alpern. 'Versification'. In *Diez comedias del Siglo de Oro*. 2nd ed. Rev. Leonard Mades. New York 1968: xxv–xxix.

Menéndez y Pelayo, Marcelino. *Calderón y su teatro*. (ed.) Carlos Marfani. Buenos Aires, 1911.

The New Princeton Encyclopedia of Poetry and Poetics. (ed.) Alex Preminger and T.V.F. Brogan. Princeton 1993.

Ortiz Lottman, Maryrica. 'The Toothsome Mouth in *El médico de su honra*'. *Bulletin of the Comediantes* 55 (2003): 87–108.

Ovid. *Metamorphoses*. (ed.) and trans. Rolfe Humphries. Bloomington, Indiana 1955.

Parker, Alexander A. *The Approach to the Spanish Drama of the Golden Age*. London 1957.

Parker, Alexander A. 'Towards a Definition of Calderonian Tragedy', *Bulletin of Hispanic Studies* 39 (1961): 222–37.

Paterson, A.K.G. Introduction. *The Painter of his Dishonour / El pintor de su deshonra*. By Pedro Calderón de la Barca. Warminster 1991: 1–18.

Perry, Mary Elizabeth. *Gender and Disorder in Early Modern Seville*. Princeton 1990.

Phillips, William D., Jr. *Slavery from Roman Times to the Early Transatlantic Trade*. Minneapolis 1985.

Randel, Mary Gaylord. 'Amor y honor a través del espejo'. In *Actas del Congreso Internacional sobre Calderón y el teatro español del Siglo de Oro (Madrid, 8–13 de junio de 1981)*. (ed.) Luciano García Lorenzo. Vol. II. Madrid 1983: 869–79.

Rogers, Daniel. ' "Tienen los celos pasos de ladrones": Silence in Calderón's *El médico de su honra'*. *Hispanic Review* 33 (1965): 273–89.

Rogers, Edith Randam. *The Perilous Hunt: Symbols in Hispanic and European Balladry*. Lexington, Kentucky 1980.

Ruano de la Haza, José María. 'Hacia una metodología para la reconstrucción de la puesta en escena de la comedia en los teatros comerciales del siglo XVII'. *Criticón* 42 (1988): 81–101.

Ruano de la Haza, José María. and John J. Allen. *Los teatros comerciales del siglo XVII y la escenificación de la comedia*. Madrid 1994.

Ruiz de Alarcón y Mendoza, Juan. *Ganar amigos*. In *Obras completas de Juan Ruiz de Alarcón II: Teatro*. (ed.) Agustín Millares Caro. México 1959: 277–362.

Shergold, N.D. *A History of the Spanish Stage*. Oxford 1967.

Shergold, N.D. and J.E. Varey. 'Some Early Calderón Dates'. *Bulletin of Hispanic Studies* 38 (1961): 274–86.

Shergold, N.D. 'Some Palace Performances of Seventeenth-Century Plays'. *Bulletin of Hispanic Studies* 40 (1963): 212–44.

Simerka, Barbara. 'The Generic Dimension of Self-Referentiality: Calderón's *El médico de su honra* as *Metadrama de Honor'*. *Bulletin of the Comediantes* 46 (1994): 103–14.

Sloman, Albert E. *The Dramatic Craftsmanship of Calderón: His Use of Earlier Plays*. Oxford 1969.

Soufas, Teresa Scott. 'Beyond Justice and Cruelty: Calderón's King Pedro'. *Journal of Hispanic Philology* 6 (1981): 57–65.

Soufas, Teresa Scott. 'Calderón's Joyless Jester: The Humanization of a Stock Character'. *Bulletin of the Comediantes* 34 (1982): 201–8.

Soufas, Teresa Scott. 'Calderón's Melancholy Wife-Murderers'. *Hispanic Review* 52 (1984): 181–203.

Soufas, Teresa Scott. 'Death and Sleep in *El médico de su honra*: Calderón's Startling Dramatization of a Poetic Tradition'. *Crítica Hispánica* 52 (1984): 61–7.

Soufas, Teresa Scott. *Melancholy and the Secular Mind in Spanish Golden Age Literature*. Columbia, Missouri 1990.

Spitzer, Leo. '"Soy Quien Soy"'. *Nueva Revista de Filología Hispánica* 1 (1948): 113–27.

Stroud, Matthew D. *Fatal Union: A Pluralistic Approach to the Spanish Wife-Murder 'Comedias'*. London 1990.

Sullivan, Henry W. *Calderón in the German Lands and the Low Countries: His Reception and Influence, 1654–1980*. Cambridge 1983.

The Times Atlas of World History. (ed.) Geoffrey Barraclough. London 1978.

Valbuena Briones, Angel. 'El emblema simbólico de la caída del caballo'. In *Calderón y la comedia nueva*. Madrid 1977: 88–105.

Valbuena Briones, Angel. (ed.) *El médico de su honra*. By Pedro Calderón de la Barca. In *Dramas de honor*. Vol II. Madrid 1970.

Vega, Lope de. *Arte nuevo de hacer comedias*. In *Preceptiva dramática española*. 2nd ed. (eds) Federico Sánchez Escribano and Alberto Porqueras Mayo. Madrid 1972: 154–65.

Vega, Lope de. *The New Art of Writing Plays*. Trans. William T. Brewster. New York 1914. Repr. in *Papers on Playmaking*. (ed.) Brander Matthews. Preface by Henry W. Wells. New York 1957.

Wardropper, Bruce W. 'The Dramatic Epilogue in Golden Age Spain'. *Modern Language Notes* 101 (1986): 205–19.

Wardropper, Bruce W. (ed.) *El médico de su honra*. By Pedro Calderón de la Barca. In *Teatro Español del Siglo de Oro*. New York 1970: 497–609.

Wardropper, Bruce W. 'Poetry and Drama in Calderón's *El médico de su honra*'. *Romanic Review* 49 (1958): 3–11.

Watson, A. Irvine. 'Peter the Cruel of Peter the Just? A Reappraisal of the Role Played by King Peter in Calderón's *El médico de su honra*'. *Romanistisches Jarhbuch* 14 (1963): 322–46.

Weissberger, Barbara F. *Isabel Rules: Constructing Queenship, Wielding Power*. Minneapolis 2004.

Wilson, E.M. 'The Four Elements in the Imagery of Calderón'. *Modern Language Review* 31 (1936): 34–47.

Wilson, E.M. 'Gerald Brenan's Calderón'. *Bulletin of the Comediantes* 6 (1952): 6–8.

Yarbro-Bejarano, Yvonne. *Feminism and the Honor Plays of Lope de Vega*. West Lafayette, Indiana 1994.

DEL MEDICO DE SU HONRA

COMEDIA FAMOSA

de don Pedro Calderón de la Barca

CONCERNING

THE PHYSICIAN OF HIS HONOUR

THE FAMOUS PLAY

by
Don Pedro Calderón de la Barca

Personas que hablan en ella	Speaking parts
DON GUTIERRE	DON GUTIERRE
DOÑA MENCÍA DE ACUÑA	DOÑA MENCÍA DE ACUÑA
EL REY DON PEDRO	KING PEDRO
DOÑA LEONOR	DOÑA LEONOR
EL INFANTE DON ENRIQUE	PRINCE ENRIQUE
UNA ESCLAVA [JACINTA]	SLAVE [JACINTA]
DON ARIAS	DON ARIAS
INES, CRIADA	INES, MAID
DON DIEGO	DON DIEGO
[TEODORA, CRIADA]	[TEODORA, MAID]
[COQUÍN, LACAYO]	[COQUÍN, LACKEY]
[LUDOVICO, SANGRADOR]	[LUDOVICO, BLOODLETTER]
[SOLDADOS]	[SOLDIERS]
[UN VIEJO]	[OLD MAN]
[*Música*]	[*Music*]

PRIMERA JORNADA

Suena ruido de caja, y sale cayendo el Infante don Enrique, y don Arias, y don Diego y algo detrás el Rey don Pedro, todos de camino.

DON ENRIQUE	¡Jesús mil veces!
DON ARIAS	¡El cielo
	te valga!
REY	¿Qué fue?
DON ARIAS	Cayó

el caballo, y arrojó
desde él al Infante al suelo.

REY   Si las torres de Sevilla   5
saluda de esa manera,
¡nunca a Sevilla viniera,
nunca dejara a Castilla!
    ¡Enrique! ¡Hermano!

DON DIEGO   ¡Señor!

REY ¿No vuelve?

DON ARIAS   A un tiempo ha perdido   10
pulso, color y sentido.
¡Qué desdicha!

DON DIEGO   ¡Qué dolor!

REY   Llegad a esa quinta bella,
que está del camino al paso,
don Arias, a ver si acaso,   15
recogido un poco en ella,
    cobra salud el Infante.
Todos os quedad aquí,
y dadme un caballo a mí,
que he de pasar adelante;   20
    que aunque este horror y mancilla
mi rémora pudo ser,
no me quiero detener
hasta llegar a Sevilla.
    Allá llegará la nueva   25
del suceso.

Vase.

ACT ONE

The sound of drums, as Prince Enrique enters, falling. He is accompanied by Don Arias and Don Diego, followed somewhat further back by King Pedro. All are dressed for travel.

PRINCE	Lord Jesus!
DON ARIAS	God help you!
KING	What happened?
DON ARIAS	The horse fell, throwing the Prince to the ground!
KING	If this is the way he greets the towers of Seville, I wish he had never come! Better never to have left Castile! Enrique! Brother!
DON DIEGO	Sir!
KING	Isn't he coming around?
DON ARIAS	He's lost all his colour, consciousness, and pulse. What a calamity!
DON DIEGO	How terrible!
KING	Don Arias, go to that country home up the road, to see if the Prince can rest and recover there. All of you stay with him, and bring me a horse, because I have to go on. Although this unhappy accident has delayed me, I mustn't stop until I reach Seville. News about him will catch up with me there.

He leaves.

1 *¡Jesús mil veces!* Literally, 'Jesus, a thousand times!'
7 *viniera* is ambiguous here because the subject of the verb is not stated: the line could also read 'I wish I had never come!'
21 *mancilla*: In archaic Spanish, 'any wound or injury that moves us to compassion' (Covarrubias, p. 731b).

DON ARIAS	Esta ocasión
	de su fiera condición
	ha sido bastante prueba.
	¿Quién a un hermano dejara,
	tropezando desta suerte 30
	en los brazos de la muerte?
	¡Vive Dios!
DON DIEGO	Calla, y repara
	en que, si oyen las paredes,
	los troncos, don Arias, ven,
	y nada nos está bien. 35
DON ARIAS	Tú, don Diego, llegar puedes
	a esa quinta; y di que aquí
	el Infante mi señor
	cayó. Pero no; mejor
	será que los dos así 40
	le llevemos donde pueda
	descansar.
DON DIEGO	Has dicho bien.
DON ARIAS	Viva Enrique, y otro bien
	la suerte no me conceda.

Llevan al Infante, y sale doña Mencía y Jacinta, esclava herrada.

DOÑA MENCÍA	Desde la torre los vi, 45
	y aunque quien son no podré
	distinguir, Jacinta, sé
	que una gran desdicha allí
	ha sucedido. Venía
	un bizarro caballero 50
	en un bruto tan ligero,
	que en el viento parecía
	un pájaro que volaba;
	y es razón que lo presumas,
	porque un penacho de plumas 55
	matices al aire daba.
	El campo y el sol en ellas
	compitieron resplandores;
	que el campo le dio sus flores,
	y el sol le dio sus estrellas; 60
	porque cambiadan de modo,
	y de modo relucían,

DON ARIAS	Well, that's proof enough of his brutality. Who'd leave a brother like that, stumbling into the arms of death? Good God!
DON DIEGO	Be quiet! Don't forget, Don Arias: if walls have ears, the trees have eyes, and nothing's safe for us.
DON ARIAS	Don Diego, go up to that house, and tell them the Prince has fallen. No – wait. It would be better for us to carry him there.
DON DIEGO	Good idea.
DON ARIAS	Please, God, don't let Enrique die.

They carry off the Prince.

[* *]*

Enter Doña Mencía and Jacinta, a branded slave.

DA. MENCÍA	I saw them from the tower, Jacinta. I can't tell who they are, but I know that something terrible has happened. A gallant knight came on a steed so swift that it seemed like a bird flying in the wind, painting the air with a crest of plumes. The splendours of the field and of the sun competed with each other in those plumes: the field sent flowers, and the sun sent stars, because the crest bloomed and shone. One moment it was the sun,

---

30 *desta suerte* = *de esta suerte.*

33–34 *si oyen las paredes, los troncos ... ven* / **if walls have eras, the trees have eyes** recalls the Spanish saying 'Las paredes han oídos, y los montes ojos' (The walls have ears and the mountains, eyes) (Correas p. 456).

44+ **branded slave**: see 'Jacinta' under 'Characters' in Introduction, and note 14.

45–72 **I saw them from the tower....** Doña Mencía's speech here is a fine example of the *culterano* style of writing at which Calderón excelled. See 'Language and Style' in Introduction.

46 *quien son* = *quienes son.*

que en todo al sol parecían,
y a la primavera en todo.

Corrió, pues, y tropezó   65
el caballo, de manera
que lo que ave entonces era,
cuando en la tierra cayó
fue rosa; y así en rigor
imitó su lucimiento   70
en sol, cielo, tierra y viento,
ave, bruto, estrella y flor.

JACINTA   ¡Ay, señora! En casa ha entrado...
DOÑA MENCÍA   ¿Quién?
JACINTA   ...un confuso tropel
de gente.
DOÑA MENCÍA   ¿Mas que con él   75
a nuestra quinta han llegado?

Salen don Arias y don Diego, y sacan al Infante, y siéntanle en una silla.

DON DIEGO   En las casas de los nobles
tiene tan divino imperio
la sangre del Rey, que ha dado
en la vuestra atrevimiento   80
para entrar desta manera.
DOÑA MENCÍA   [*Ap.*] ¿Qué es esto que miro? ¡Ay cielos!
DON DIEGO   El Infante don Enrique,
hermano del Rey don Pedro,
a vuestras puertas cayó,   85
y llega aquí medio muerto.
DOÑA MENCÍA   ¡Válgame Dios, qué desdicha!
DON ARIAS   Decidnos a qué aposento
podrá retirarse, en tanto
que vuelva al primero aliento   90
su vida. ¿Pero qué miro?
¡Señora!
DOÑA MENCÍA   ¡Don Arias!
DON ARIAS   Creo
que es sueño fingido cuanto
estoy escuchando y viendo.
¿Que el Infante don Enrique,   95
más amante que primero,
vuelva a Sevilla, y te halle

and the next, it was a spring meadow.

When the galloping horse stumbled, the bird fell to the earth and became a rose. And so in its brilliance the crest simulated the sun, sky, earth, and wind; bird, brute, star and flower.

JACINTA	Oh, my lady! They've come into the house!
DA. MENCÍA	Who?
JACINTA	Those people you saw.
DA. MENCÍA	They've brought him here?

Enter Don Arias and Don Diego. They carry the Prince and seat him on a chair.

DON DIEGO	Madam, we brought him into your noble home because he's a member of the royal family.
DA. MENCÍA	*[Aside]* Good heavens, what's this I see?
DON DIEGO	Prince Enrique, the King's brother, fell at your door, and here he is, half dead.
DA. MENCÍA	My God, how unfortunate!
DON ARIAS	Tell us where we can take him to lie down, so he can recover. But what's this? Madame!
DA. MENCÍA	Don Arias!
DON ARIAS	I must be dreaming. Can it be that the Prince, coming back to Seville and more in love than ever, finds you this way?

---

90 *aliento* 'vigor of the soul, strength, and valour' (*Diccionario de Autoridades*, I, p. 212b). *Primero aliento* may also mean 'first breath'.

	con tan infeliz encuentro, puede ser verdad?	
DOÑA MENCÍA	Sí, es; ¡y ojalá que fuera sueño!	100
DON ARIAS	Pues ¿qué haces aquí?	
DOÑA MENCÍA	De espacio lo sabrás; que ahora no es tiempo sino sólo de acudir a la vida de tu dueño.	
DON ARIAS	¿Quién le dijera que así llegara a verte?	105
DOÑA MENCÍA	Silencio, que importa mucho, don Arias.	
DON ARIAS	¿Por qué?	
DOÑA MENCÍA	Va mi honor en ello. Entrad en ese retiro, donde está un catre cubierto de un cuero turco y de flores; y en él, aunque humilde lecho, podrá descansar. Jacinta, saca tú ropa al momento, aguas y olores que sean dignos de tan alto empleo.	110 115

Vase Jacinta.

DON ARIAS	Los dos, mientras se adereza, aquí al Infante dejemos, y a su remedio acudamos, si hay en desdichas remedio.	 120

Vanse los dos.

DOÑA MENCÍA	Ya se fueron, ya he quedado sola. ¡O quién pudiera, ah, cielos, con licencia de su honor hacer aquí sentimientos! ¡O quién pudiera dar voces, y romper con el silencio cárceles de nieve, donde está aprisionado el fuego, que ya, resuelto en cenizas, es ruina que está diciendo:	 125 130

DA. MENCÍA	Yes, it's true, and I wish it were a dream!
DON ARIAS	Well, what are you doing here?
DA. MENCÍA	I'll tell you later. Now we've got to take care of your master.
DON ARIAS	Who would have thought that he'd come back to you like this?
DA. MENCÍA	Please, keep quiet about this, Don Arias.
DON ARIAS	Why?
DA. MENCÍA	My honour depends on it. Take him into that room, where there's a simple cot covered with Turkish leather and flowers. He can rest and recover there. Jacinta, run get the bedclothes, and fix up the room with water and perfumes for our honoured guest.

Jacinta leaves.

DON ARIAS	[*to Don Diego*] While they're getting it ready, let's leave the Prince here, and seek a remedy for him – if there is any.

They leave.

DA. MENCÍA	They're gone now. I'm alone. Oh, heavens, if only my honour allowed me to show my feelings! Oh, if only I could cry out, shattering the frozen silence with the fire imprisoned in my heart! But now it's just a ruin, ashes saying, 'Love used to dwell here'.

101 *De espacio* = *despacio*.

'Aquí fue amor'! Mas ¿qué digo?
¿Qué es esto, cielos, qué es esto?
Yo soy quien soy. Vuelva el aire
los repetidos acentos
que llevó; porque aun perdidos,   135
no es bien que publiquen ellos
lo que yo debo callar,
porque ya, con más acuerdo,
ni para sentir soy mía;
y solamente me huelgo   140
de tener hoy que sentir,
por tener en mis deseos
que vencer; pues no hay virtud
sin experiencia. Perfeto
está el oro en el crisol,   145
el imán en el acero,
el diamante en el diamante,
los metales en el fuego:
y así mi honor en sí mismo
se acrisola, cuando llego   150
a vencerme, pues no fuera
sin experiencias perfeto.
¡Piedad, divinos cielos!
¡Viva callando, pues callando muero!
¡Enrique! ¡Señor!

DON ENRIQUE   ¿Quién llama?   155
DOÑA MENCÍA   ¡Albricias…

But what am I saying? What is this, heavens, what's going on? I am who I am. I take back what I just said – my honour's not safe if I put into words what I should never say. Yes, I've got to think, because I'm not allowed to feel anymore: I belong to someone else.

And today I'm glad to have something to feel, if only for the chance to crush those desires. Virtue doesn't exist until it's tested and proven. Gold is proven perfect in the crucible; a magnet in contact with steel; a diamond against a diamond; and metals in fire. My honour is purified when I conquer myself: it wouldn't be perfect without a test.

Heaven help me! Keeping this inside is killing me! But I must go on, keeping it inside!

Enrique! Sir!

PRINCE	Who is it?
DA. MENCÍA	Thank goodness –

131 *Aquí fue amor* / **Love used to dwell here:** Mencía echoes the Spanish saying 'Here was Troy' (*Aquí fue Troya*). She refers literally to the destruction of the ancient city at the hands of the invading Greeks, and figuratively to the demolition of her great passion for the prince. At this point Calderón indirectly associates Enrique with Aeneas, the prince of Troy who escaped the devastation of his city, eventually to found Rome. Virgil tells the epic story in the *Aeneid*. See also lines 240–2.

133 *Yo soy quien soy* / **I am who I am:** A statement defining identity that occurs repeatedly in Calderón's *comedias*, particularly when noble characters (often wives in the so-called 'honour dramas') find themselves in circumstances that test their resolve to maintain their integrity. **I am who I am** may be taken as a declaration that 'I know my station (personal, social, religious) and I intend to uphold it'. Spitzer relates the phrase to God's self-definition in Genesis. See also Casa, p. 41.

In the romantic comedy *Love Is No Laughing Matter* (*No hay burlas con el amor*), Calderón parodies his own device. There the comic servant Inés is pursued by and flirts with the aristocrat Don Alonso, whose intention toward her is seduction rather than marriage. However, she actually loves his servant Moscatel. The latter is charged with conveying his master's attraction to Inés, who indignantly replies, 'Tell your master, wretch, that I am who I am; that he needn't entertain any fancy notions about me ...', II, 1257–9).

138 *acuerdo*: Can mean 'deliberation or resolution taken with maturity and knowledge' (*Autoridades* I, 73b).

144 *Perfeto* = *perfecto*.

DON ENRIQUE	¡Válgame el cielo!
DOÑA MENCÍA	…que vive tu Alteza!
DON ENRIQUE	¿Dónde

estoy?

DOÑA MENCÍA   En parte, a lo menos,
donde de vuestra salud
hay quien se huelgue.

DON ENRIQUE   Lo creo,   160
si esta dicha, por ser mía,
no se deshace en el viento,
pues consultando conmigo
estoy, si despierto sueño,
o si dormido discurro,   165
pues a un tiempo duermo y velo.
Pero ¿para qué averiguo,
poniendo a mayores riesgos
la verdad? Nunca despierte,
si es verdad que agora duermo;   170
y nunca duerma en mi vida,
si es verdad que estoy despierto.

DOÑA MENCÍA Vuestra Alteza, gran señor,
trate prevenido y cuerdo
de su salud, cuya vida   175
dilate siglos eternos,
fénix de su misma fama,
imitando al que en el fuego
ave, llama, ascua y gusano,
urna, pira, voz y incendio   180
nace, vive, dura y muere,
hijo y padre de sí mesmo;
que después sabrá de mí
dónde está.

DON ENRIQUE   No lo deseo;
que si estoy vivo y te miro,   185
ya mayor dicha no espero;
ni mayor dicha tampoco,
si te miro estando muerto;
pues es fuerza que sea gloria
donde vive ángel tan bello.   190
Y así no quiero saber
qué acasos ni qué sucesos

PRINCE	Good God!
DA. MENCÍA	– Your Highness is alive!
PRINCE	Where am I?
DA. MENCÍA	Where someone is more than glad to see you on the mend.
PRINCE	I believe it – if this good luck of mine doesn't blow away in the wind. I'm wondering if I've awakened from a dream, or if I'm talking in my sleep: or perhaps I'm asleep and awake at the same time. But why do I even ask, since that would risk destroying this lovely dream? If I'm really asleep now, may I never awaken, and if I'm really awake let me never sleep again.
DA. MENCÍA	Sir, Your Highness must rest now – take good care of your health, and live on for centuries. Be like the phoenix, imitate the mythical creature, the bird, flame, ember, and worm, the urn, pyre, voice and fire who is born, lives, and dies, father and son to himself. I'll tell you where you are later.
PRINCE	But I don't want to know. If I'm alive and looking at you, it's all I could ever hope for; and if I'm dead and see you, what more could I want? Because where such a lovely angel lives must be heaven. So I don't want to know what chances or what

---

157–9   *que vive tu Alteza ... vuestra salud*: Here Mencía's address of the Prince shifts between the intimate 'tú' and the more formal 'vuestra' (as in "Vuestra Alteza', line 173). The switch may be attributed to mixed feelings and disquiet, or alternatively to the exigencies of versification. Similar inconsistencies of address occur throughout the play, for example in Mencía and Gutierre's conversation later in the first Act (495–554), mingling 'tú' and 'vos'); again in Act II in Mencía's speech to the Prince (1098–135); as well as the beginning of Act III in the conversations of Gutierre with the King and then Enrique with the King.

170   *agora* = *ahora*.

177   **phoenix**: 'A mythical bird, of gorgeous plumage, fabled to be the only one of its kind, and to live five or six hundred years in the Arabian desert, after which it burnt itself to ashes on a funeral pyre of aromatic twigs ignited by the sun and fanned by its own wings, but only to emerge form its ashes with renewed youth, to live through another cycle of years'. One version of the myth held that 'a worm emerged from the ashes and became the young phoenix'. Speaking figuratively, a **phoenix** may be 'a person (or thing) of unique excellence or of matchless beauty; a paragon' (*Oxford English Dictionary*).

180   *y incendio*: The combination 'y + i-' was common in Golden Age Spanish.

182   *mesmo* = *mismo* (*mesmo* preserves the assonant rhyme with *incendio* [180] and *deseo* [184]).

	aquí mi vida guiaron,	
	ni aquí la tuya trujeron;	
	pues con saber que estoy donde	195
	estás tú, vivo contento;	
	y así, ni tú que decirme,	
	ni yo que escucharte tengo.	
DOÑA MENCÍA	([*Ap.*] Presto de tantos favores	
	será desengaño el tiempo.)	200
	Dígame ahora, ¿cómo está	
	vuestra Alteza?	
DON ENRIQUE	Estoy tan bueno,	
	que nunca estuve mejor;	
	sólo en esta pierna siento	
	un dolor.	
DOÑA MENCÍA	Fue gran caída;	205
	pero en descansando, pienso	
	que cobraréis la salud;	
	y ya os están previniendo	
	cama donde descanséis.	
	Que me perdonéis, os ruego,	210
	la humildad de la posada;	
	aunque disculpada quedo…	
DON ENRIQUE	Muy como señora habláis,	
	Mencía. ¿Sois vos el dueño	
	desta casa?	
DOÑA MENCÍA	No, señor;	215
	pero de quien lo es, sospecho	
	que lo soy.	
DON ENRIQUE	Y ¿quien lo es?	
DOÑA MENCÍA	Un ilustre caballero	
	Gutierre Alfonso Solís,	
	mi esposo y esclavo vuestro.	220
DON ENRIQUE	¿Vuestro esposo?	

[Levántase.]

DOÑA MENCÍA	Sí, señor.	
	No os levantéis, deteneos;	
	ved que no podéis estar	
	en pie.	
DON ENRIQUE	Sí puedo, sí puedo.	

Sale don Arias.

	accidents brought either of us here. I'm content just knowing I'm with you. So you don't have to tell me anything, nor I to listen.
DA. MENCÍA	([*Aside*] Soon enough he'll find out that all those pretty words are wasted.) Tell me now, Your Highness, how do you feel?
PRINCE	I've never been better – just this leg hurts a little.
DA. MENCÍA	You took a bad fall, but if you rest, I think you'll feel better. Now they're fixing a bed where you can rest. I hope you'll forgive the poor accommodations, although I have an excuse –
PRINCE	Mencía, you sound like the lady of the house. Are you its mistress?
DA. MENCÍA	No, sir, but I am of its master.
PRINCE	And who is that?
DA. MENCÍA	A distinguished knight, Gutierre Alfonso Solís, my husband and your servant.
PRINCE	Your husband?

[He rises.]

| DA. MENCÍA | Yes, sir. Stop, don't get up! Look, you can't stand up! |
| PRINCE | Yes, I can, I can! |

Enter Don Arias.

---

194 *trujeron* = *trajeron*.

214 *dueño*: 'the male owner who has dominion over something: and also the woman and other objects of the female gender that have dominion over something are called [*dueño*]; in order not to call them "dueñas", a word that is now [1724] commonly understood as meaning maids of honour' (*Autoridades* II, p. 348b). See also lines 495 and 2036.

DON ARIAS	Dame, gran señor, las plantas,	225
	que mil veces toco y beso,	
	agradecido a la dicha	
	que en tu salud nos ha vuelto	
	la vida a todos.	

Sale don Diego.

DON DIEGO	Ya puede	
	vuestra Alteza a ese aposento	230
	retirarse, donde está	
	prevenido todo aquello	
	que pudo en la fantasía	
	bosquejar el pensamiento.	
DON ENRIQUE	Don Arias, dame un caballo;	235
	dame un caballo, don Diego.	
	Salgamos presto de aquí.	
DON ARIAS	¿Qué decís?	
DON ENRIQUE	Que me deis presto	
	un caballo.	
DON DIEGO	Pues, señor…	
DON ARIAS	Mira…	
DON ENRIQUE	Estáse Troya ardiendo,	240
	y Eneas de mis sentidos,	
	he de librarlos del fuego.	

[Vase don Diego.]

¡Ay, don Arias, la caída
no fue acaso, sino agüero
de mi muerte! [*A doña Mencía*] Y con razón,   245
pues fue divino decreto
que viniese a morir yo,
con tan justo sentimiento,
donde tú estabas casada,
porque nos diesen a un tiempo   250
pésames y parabienes
de tu boda y de mi entierro.
De verse el bruto a tu sombra,
pensé que, altivo y soberbio,
engendró con osadía   255
bizarros atrevimientos,
cuando presumiendo de ave,

DON ARIAS	My Lord, thank goodness! If you're better, then all is well.

Enter Don Diego.

DON DIEGO	Your Highness, the room's ready now, fit for a prince; do go and rest.
PRINCE	Get me a horse, Don Arias. Don Diego, get me a horse. Let's get out of here.
DON ARIAS	What?
PRINCE	I said, get me a horse!
DON DIEGO	But, sir –
DON ARIAS	Look –
PRINCE	Can't you see that Troy's burning? I'm another Aeneas, and I've got to save my feelings from the fire.

[Don Diego leaves.]

Ah, Don Arias, that fall was no accident; it was an omen of my death! [*To Doña Mencía*] And no wonder, because heaven has decreed that when you married, I should die. They can congratulate you and mourn me, for your wedding and my funeral.

When my horse, the haughty and arrogant brute, found itself in your shadow, I thought he dared to fly. Like a bird, he vanquished the winds, and then, neighing for combat,

---

240–2 **Aeneas** saved his father and son from Troy as it burned. See line 131 note.
245 [*A doña Mencía*] / [*To Doña Mencía*] We have added this stage direction.
250 *Porque* = *para que.*

con relinchos cuerpo a cuerpo
desafiaba los rayos,
despés que venció los vientos;   260
y no fue sino que al ver
tu casa, montes de celos
se le pusieron delante,
porque tropezase en ellos;
que aun un bruto se desboca   265
con celos; y no hay tan diestro
jinete, que allí no pierda
los estribos al correrlos.
Milagro de tu hermosura
presumí el feliz suceso   270
de mi vida, pero ya,
más desengañado, pienso
que no fue sino venganza
de mi muerte; pues es cierto
que muero, y que no hay milagros   275
que se examinen muriendo.

DOÑA MENCÍA Quien oyere a vuestra Alteza
quejas, agravios, desprecios,
podrá formar de mi honor
presunciones y concetos   280
indignos dél; y yo agora,
por si acaso llevó el viento
cabal alguna razón,
sin que en partidos acentos
la troncase, responder   285
a tantos agravios quiero,
porque donde fueron quejas,
vayan con el mismo aliento
desengaños. Vuestra Alteza,
liberal de sus deseos,   290
generoso de sus gustos,
pródigo de sus afectos,
puso los ojos en mí:
es verdad, yo lo confieso.
Bien sabe, de tantos años   295
de experiencias, el respeto
con que constante mi honor
fue una montaña de hielo,

he challenged the rays of the sun itself.

But it was simply that when he saw your house, mountains of jealousy rose up in his path so that he'd stumble over them. Even a brute can run wild with jealousy, and even the most skilled horseman will lose his stirrups when he races with jealousy.

I thought your beauty was a miracle, and beholding it the happiest moment of my life. But now I see the truth. Now I think it was some kind of revenge, and it will kill me, because I tell you, I'm dying. When a man dies, not even a miracle can save him.

DA. MENCÍA   Anyone hearing Your Highness speak this way would think badly of my honour. Just in case the wind carried off to others any of your complaints, I'll answer you. Let the same wind convey my explanation.

Your Highness, liberal in your desires and lavish in your affections, saw me one day, and you wanted me. It's true, I admit it. And you know very well, from so many years of trying, that my honour resisted you. I was a mountain

---

277   *oyere*: future subjunctive (not used in modern Spanish).

281   *dél = de él.*

289   *desengaños*: On the significance of *desengaño* in Golden Age literature, see Otis H. Green IV, pp. 42–76. Mencía uses the term here in the sense of 'liberation from error' (p. 73).

291   *generoso*: 'The illustrious man, born of very noble parents, and of impeccable lineage, known by his family tree. 1. He is generous by lineage. 2. Generous at times means he who, in terms of his person alone, has worth and virtue, a noble, liberal, and generous condition' (Covarrubias, p. 586a).

289–92 Your Highness, liberal in your desires … Here Mencía appears to imply that the Prince eventually succeeded in seducing her. However, the remainder of this speech gives us to understand that she did not yield to him.

conquistada de las flores,
escuadrones que arma el tiempo.   300
Si me casé, ¿de qué engaño
se queja, siendo sujeto
imposible a sus pasiones,
reservado a sus intentos,
pues soy para dama más,   305
lo que para esposa menos?
Y así, en esta parte ya
disculpada, en la que tengo
de mujer, a vuestros pies
humilde, señor, os ruego   310
no os ausentéis desta casa,
poniendo a tan claro riesgo
la salud.

DON ENRIQUE   ¡Cuánto mayor
en esta casa le tengo!

Salen don Gutierre Alfonso y Coquín.

DON GUTIERRE   Déme los pies vuestra Alteza,   315
si puedo de tanto sol
tocar, ¡o rayo español!,
la majestad y grandeza.
Con alegría y tristeza
hoy a vuestras plantas llego,   320
y mi aliento, lince y ciego,
entre asombros y desmayos,
es águila a tantos rayos,
mariposa a tanto fuego:
tristeza de la caída   325
que puso con triste efeto
a Castilla en tanto aprieto;
y alegría de la vida
que vuelve restituida
a su pompa, a su belleza,   330
cuando en gusto vuestra Alteza
trueca ya la pena mía.
¿Quién vio triste la alegría?,
¿quién vio alegre la tristeza?
Y honrad por tan breve espacio   335
esta esfera, aunque pequeña;

of ice, conquered with flowers, squadrons armed by time.

If I married, how can you complain of deception? I was never meant for you. I was beyond your reach, since I'm too noble to be your lover, and not noble enough to be your wife.

So now that I've explained myself, let me speak simply as a woman: sir, I beg you not to leave this house – it would be too great a risk to your health.

PRINCE   Oh, but the risk is so much greater if I stay!

Enter Don Gutierre Alfonso and Coquín.

DON GUTIERRE Your Highness, let me kiss your feet, if I may be so bold, oh Spanish ray of light, as to touch the person of your great majesty.

I arrive both joyful and sad, and my spirit, both lynx-eyed and blind, among frights and faints, is like an eagle to so many rays of light, a moth to such a flame.

I'm sad at the fall that nearly cost Castile so dearly; and filled with joy that Your Majesty has come back to life to take up once again your rightful pomp and splendour: my sorrow turns to pleasure. How could there be sadness in joy? How could there be joy in sadness?

Please honour my sphere for a time, however brief. After all,

porque el sol no se desdeña,
despés que ilustró un palacio,
de iluminar el topacio
de algún pajizo arrebol.   340
Y pues sois rayo español,
descansad aquí; que es ley
hacer el palacio el rey
también, si hace esfera el sol.

DON ENRIQUE   El gusto y pesar estimo   345
del modo que le sentís,
Gutierre Alfonso Solís;
y así en el alma le imprimo,
donde a tenerle me animo
guardado.

DON GUTIERRE   Sabe tu Alteza   350
honrar.

DON ENRIQUE   Y aunque la grandeza
desta casa fuera aquí
grande esfera para mí,
pues lo fue de otra belleza,
    no me puedo detener;   355
que pienso que esta caída
ha de costarme la vida;
y no sólo por caer,
sino también por hacer
que no pasase adelante   360
mi intento: y es importante
irme; que hasta un desengaño
cada minuto es un año,
es un siglo cada instante.

DON GUTIERRE   Señor, ¿vuestra Alteza tiene   365
causa tal, que su inquietud
aventure la salud
de una vida que previene
tantos aplausos?

DON ENRIQUE   Conviene
llegar a Sevilla hoy.   370

DON GUTIERRE Necio en apurar estoy
vuestro intento; pero creo
que mi lealtad y deseo...

DON ENRIQUE Y si yo la causa os doy,
    ¿qué diréis?

the sun, having illuminated a palace, condescends to shine on the topaz of a rose-coloured and straw-thatched cottage. And since you're a Spanish ray of light, rest here. If the sun creates its own sphere, the king also makes his own palace.

PRINCE   I appreciate your pleasure and pain, Gutierre Alfonso Solís; they're impressed upon my soul.

DON GUTIERRE   Your Highness honours me.

PRINCE   And even if this fine house were a palace for me, as it has been for one beauty, I couldn't stay. I think this fall is going to cost me my life. Not just because of the accident, but for ruining my plans. I must go: until I can learn the truth, each minute is a year to me, each second lasts a century.

DON GUTIERRE   Sir, is Your Majesty's reason to leave so pressing that it would cause you to risk your most illustrious life?

PRINCE   I must get to Seville today.

DON GUTIERRE   I know it's presumptuous of me to question why, but I think my loyalty and desire –

PRINCE   And if I tell you why, what will you say?

315–44 Your Highness, let me kiss your feet ... 'In the geocentric system of the universe, each of the major stars had its own sphere in which it revolved; metaphorically, the sphere of a prince such as Don Enrique (the sun) is a palace, but the sun also lends its light to the topaz (a semiprecious stone, that symbolizes Don Gutierre's country home). Furthermore, the site where a king rests is effectively a palace' (Cruickshank 1989, p. 90).

DON GUTIERRE	Yo no os la pido;	375
	que a vos, señor, no es bien hecho	
	examinaros el pecho.	
DON ENRIQUE	Pues escuchad: yo he tenido	
	un amigo tal, que ha sido	
	otro yo.	
DON GUTIERRE	Dichoso fue.	380
DON ENRIQUE	A éste en mi ausencia fié	
	el alma, la vida, el gusto	
	en una mujer. ¿Fue justo	
	que, atropellando la fe	
	que debió al respeto mío,	385
	faltase en ausencia?	
DON GUTIERRE	No.	
DON ENRIQUE	Pues a otro dueño le dio	
	llaves de aquel albedrío;	
	al pecho que yo le fío,	
	introdujo otro señor;	390
	otro goza su favor.	
	¿Podrá un hombre enamorado	
	sosegar con tal cuidado,	
	descansar con tal dolor?	
DON GUTIERRE	No, señor.	
DON ENRIQUE	Cuando los cielos	395
	tanto me fatigan hoy,	
	que en cualquier parte que estoy,	
	estoy mirando mis celos,	
	tan presentes mis desvelos	
	están delante de mí,	400
	que aquí los miro, y así	
	de aquí ausentarme deseo;	
	que aunque van conmigo, creo	
	que se han de quedar aquí.	
DOÑA MENCÍA	Dicen que el primer consejo	405
	ha de ser de la mujer;	
	y así, señor, quiero ser	
	(perdonad si os aconsejo)	
	quien os dé consuelo. Dejo	
	aparte celos, y digo	410
	que aguardéis a vuestro amigo,	
	hasta ver si se disculpa;	

DON GUTIERRE I'm not asking you, sir; it's not my place to examine your heart.

PRINCE Well, listen: I had such a good friend that he was a second self to me.

DON GUTIERRE He was fortunate.

PRINCE While I was away, I entrusted to him my soul, my life, my joy: a woman. Is it right that breaking his word, he betrayed me while I was gone?

DON GUTIERRE No.

PRINCE Well, he gave the keys of her free will to someone else; he introduced another lord into the heart that belonged to me; she favours someone else now. Can a man in love sit back and accept this? Should I suffer and do nothing?

DON GUTIERRE No, sir.

PRINCE What a terrible day. The stars are aligned against me. This is unbearable: here everywhere I look I see my jealousy, so I've got to get away. I can't shake my jealous thoughts. I want to leave them behind, but I know they'll go with me.

DA. MENCÍA Sir, they say that you should listen to a woman's advice first of all, so if you'll pardon my presumption, I'd like to offer you some consolation. Leaving aside for a moment your jealousy, I suggest that you speak with your friend to see if he has an explanation. Sometimes things happen

---

388 *albedrío* / **free will:** This term is repeated twice in the next 110 lines (see lines 418 and 498) and appears nowhere else in the play.

405–6 They say that the first advice …: Proverbially, a woman's advice should be heard first: *De la mujer, el consejo primero; del hombre, el postrero* (From a woman, the first advice; from a man, the last); and *De la mujer, el primer consejo; el segundo no le quiero* (From a woman, the first advice; I'll want no second) (Cruickshank 1989, p. 93).

que hay calidades de culpa
que no merecen castigo.
   No os despeñe vuestro brío;   415
mirad, aunque estéis celoso,
que ninguno es poderoso
en el ajeno albedrío.
   Cuanto al amigo, confío
que os he respondido ya;   420
cuanto a la dama, quizá
fuerza, y no mudanza fue:
oídla vos, que yo sé
que ella se disculpará.

DON ENRIQUE   No es posible.

[Sale don Diego.]

DON DIEGO   Ya está allí   425
el caballo apercibido.

DON GUTIERRE Si es del que hoy habéis caído,
no subáis en él, y aquí
recibid, señor, de mí,
una pía hermosa y bella,   430
a quien una palma sella,
signo que vuestra la hace;
que también un bruto nace
con mala o con buena estrella.
   Es este prodigio, pues,   435
proporcionado y bien hecho,
dilatado de anca y pecho;
de cabeza y cuello es
corto, de brazos y pies
fuerte, a uno y otro elemento   440
les da en sí lugar y asiento,
siendo el bruto de la palma
tierra el cuerpo, fuego el alma,
mar la espuma, y todo viento.

DON ENRIQUE   El alma aquí no podría   445
distinguir lo que procura,
la pía de la pintura,
o por mejor bizarría,
la pintura de la pía.

outside one's control. Don't let your feelings trip you up; look: although you're jealous, nobody can control someone else's free will.

Now, as far as your friend is concerned, I believe I've answered you. As for the lady, perhaps it was force and not fickleness. Listen to her, because I'm sure she'll have a good explanation.

PRINCE   It's not possible.

[Enter Don Diego.]

DON DIEGO   The horse is ready now.

DON GUTIERRE   If it's the one you fell from today, don't take him. Here, sir, let me give you a beautiful spotted mare, painted with the shape of a palm, a sign of victory that makes her yours. A brute also can be lucky, or not.

This wonderful creature is well-proportioned, with a broad haunch and chest; a fine head and neck; strong legs and hooves. The palm-printed beast carries the four elements: her body is the earth; her soul is fire; she is the sea's foam; and galloping, she takes to the wind.

PRINCE   From your splendid description, I couldn't tell which was more brilliant, the painted mare herself, or the way you've painted her in words.

---

430   *pía* / **spotted mare:** '*Pía.* Small spotted mare; they come from the islands of the north, and are for kings and great lords. The name is from the land and language of their origin' (Covarrubias, p. 820b).

431   *a quien una palma sella* / **painted [marked] with the shape of a palm:** *Palma* could mean palm of the hand, or palm tree.

432   **a sign that makes her yours:** 'A palm tree is an emblem of victory' (Covarrubias, p. 797b).

COQUÍN	Aquí entro yo. A mí me dé	450
	vuestra Alteza mano o pie,	
	lo que está (que esto es más llano),	
	o más a pie, o más a mano.	
DON GUTIERRE	Aparta, necio.	
DON ENRIQUE	¿Por qué?	
	Dejalde, su humor le abona.	455
COQUÍN	En hablando de la pía,	
	entra la persona mía,	
	que es su segunda persona.	
DON ENRIQUE	Pues ¿quién sois?	
COQUÍN	¿No lo pregona	
	mi estilo? Yo soy, en fin,	460
	Coquín, hijo de Coquín,	
	de aquesta casa escudero,	
	de la pía despensero,	
	pues le siso al celemín	
	la mitad de la comida;	465
	y en efeto, señor, hoy,	
	por ser vuestro día, os doy	
	norabuena muy cumplida.	
DON ENRIQUE	¿Mi día?	
COQUÍN	Es cosa sabida.	
DON ENRIQUE	Su día llama uno aquel	470
	que es a sus gustos fiel,	
	y lo fue a la pena mía:	
	¿cómo pudo ser mi día?	
COQUÍN	Cayendo, señor, en él;	
	y para que se publique	475
	en cuantos lunarios hay,	
	desde hoy diré: 'A tantos cay	
	San Infante don Enrique'.	
DON GUTIERRE	Tu Alteza, señor, aplique	
	la espuela al ijar; que el día	480
	ya en la tumba helada y fría,	
	huésped del undoso dios,	
	hace noche.	
DON ENRIQUE	Guárdeos Dios,	
	hermosísima Mencía;	
	y porque veáis que estimo	485
	el consejo, buscaré	

COQUÍN	This is my cue. Your Highness, give me your hand or your foot, whichever is (obviously) handier, or footier.
DON GUTIERRE	Go away, fool.
PRINCE	Why? Let him stay. I like his sense of humour.
COQUÍN	Speaking of the mare, that's my cue – because I look after her.
PRINCE	Well, who are you?
COQUÍN	Can't you guess? I'm Coquín, son of Coquín, squire of this house, steward of the mare (and I filch half the meal from her feed). Furthermore, sir, since today is your day, I give you the heartiest congratulations.
PRINCE	My day?
COQUÍN	It's obvious.
PRINCE	We call it our day if something wonderful has happened, but this one has been painful to me: how could it be my day?
COQUÍN	By falling on it, sir; and it should be published in all the almanacs: 'On such-and-such a day falls Saint Prince Don Enrique'.
DON GUTIERRE	Your Highness, it's time to apply spur to flank, for the day is now in its cold and icy tomb, guest of the briny god Neptune: the night falls.
PRINCE	May God keep you, loveliest Mencía. So you'll see how much I value your advice, I'll look for that lady, and I'll hear what she

---

455 *Dejalde* = *dejadle.*

477 *cay* = *cae.*

478 **Saint Prince Don Enrique:** Henry II, an eleventh-century German king and Holy Roman Emperor, 'became the ideal conception of the Middle Ages and can be regarded as the model Christian ruler' (*New Catholic Encyclopedia*, VI, p. 1031a). Called 'the Pious', he was lame in one leg, and known for his ability to accept counsel from subordinates, as well as for his life-long celibacy, despite having married.

480–3 **the day is now in its cold ... the night falls:** 'That is to say, the sun is setting in the ocean, dwelling of the god Neptune' (Cruickshank 1989, p. 96).

a esta dama, y della oiré
la disculpa. ([*Ap.*] Mal reprimo
el dolor, cuando me animo
a no decir lo que callo.   490
Lo que en este lance hallo,
ganar y perder se llama;
pues él me ganó la dama,
y yo le gané el caballo.)

Vase el Infante, don Arias y don Diego y Coquín.

DON GUTIERRE   Bellísimo dueño mío,   495
ya que vive tan unida
a dos almas una vida,
dos vidas a un albedrío,
de tu amor y ingenio fío
hoy, que licencia me des   500
para ir a besar los pies
al Rey mi señor, que viene
de Castilla; y le conviene
a quien caballero es,
        irle a dar la bienvenida.   505
Y fuera desto, ir sirviendo
al Infante Enrique, entiendo
que es acción justa y debida,
ya que debí a su caída
el honor que hoy ha ganado   510
nuestra casa.
DOÑA MENCÍA   ¿Qué cuidado
más te lleva a darme enojos?
DON GUTIERRE No otra cosa, ¡por tus ojos!
DOÑA MENCÍA ¿Quién duda que haya causado
        algún deseo Leonor?   515
DON GUTIERRE ¿Eso dices? No la nombres.
DOÑA MENCÍA ¡O qué tales sois los hombres!
Hoy olvido, ayer amor;
ayer gusto, y hoy rigor.
DON GUTIERRE Ayer, como al sol no vía,   520
hermosa me parecía
la luna; mas hoy, que adoro
al sol, ni dudo ni ignoro
lo que hay de la noche al día.

has to say. ([*Aside*] I must keep quiet for now about this deep pain of mine. I've both won and lost in this turn of events: he won the lady from me, and I won from him the horse.)

The Prince, Don Arias, Don Diego, and Coquín leave.

DON GUTIERRE   My most beautiful mistress, since our two souls are joined together in a single life, and our two lives in a single will, I trust that you love me enough to allow me to go properly to greet my lord the King, who's come from Castile. It's only fitting for a knight to welcome him. I should also offer my service to Prince Enrique, since I owe to his fall the honour that our house has won today.

DA. MENCÍA   What other interest that you don't mention takes you there?

DON GUTIERRE   None at all, I swear!

DA. MENCÍA   No doubt you want to see Leonor.

DON GUTIERRE   You think so? Don't even say her name.

DA. MENCÍA   Oh, you men are all the same. Yesterday you loved, today you forget; yesterday was all pleasure and today, disdain.

DON GUTIERRE   Yesterday, when I hadn't yet seen the sun, the moon seemed beautiful to me; but today, I adore the sun. Now I understand the difference between night and day.

---

494   **I won from him the horse:** Amezcua (pp. 64–7) notes the dramatic irony of the gift of the mare (i.e., the wife). He also remarks on the instability of its gender in this scene, because here Enrique refers to the animal as *caballo*, implying that it is a male horse (see line 430 note).

512   *cuidado* can mean 'love interest'.

520   *vía* = *veía*.

	Y escúchame un argumento:	525
	una llama en noche obscura	
	arde hermosa, luce pura,	
	cuyos rayos, cuyo aliento	
	dulce ilumina del viento	
	la esfera; sale el farol	530
	del cielo, y a su arrebol	
	toda a sombra se reduce;	
	ni arde, ni alumbra, ni luce,	
	que es mar de rayos el sol.	
	Aplico agora: yo amaba	535
	una luz, cuyo esplendor	
	bebió planeta mayor,	
	que sus rayos sepultaba:	
	una llama me alumbraba;	
	pero era una llama aquélla,	540
	que eclipsas divina y bella,	
	siendo de luces crisol;	
	porque hasta que sale el sol,	
	parece hermosa una estrella.	
DOÑA MENCÍA	¡Qué lisonjero os escucho!	545
	Muy parabólico estáis.	
DON GUTIERRE	En fin, ¿licencia me dais?	
DOÑA MENCÍA	Pienso que la deseáis mucho;	
	por eso cobarde lucho	
	conmigo.	
DON GUTIERRE	¿Puede en los dos	550
	haber engaño, si en vos	
	quedo yo, y vos vais en mí?	
DOÑA MENCÍA	Pues, como os quedáis aquí,	
	adiós, don Gutierre.	
DON GUTIERRE	Adiós.	

Vase don Gutierre. [Sale Jacinta.]

JACINTA	Triste, señora, has quedado.	555
DOÑA MENCÍA	Sí, Jacinta, y con razón.	
JACINTA	No sé qué nueva ocasión	
	te ha suspendido y turbado;	
	que una inquietud, un cuidado	
	te ha divertido.	
DOÑA MENCÍA	Es así.	560

Listen: on a dark night, a flame burns beautifully, shining pure. Its beams glow sweetly and flicker in the breeze. When that dazzling sphere rises in the sky, its rosy brilliance reduces everything else to shadow: then nothing else burns, lights, or glows, because the sun is a vast ocean of light.

Now I'll apply it: the great sun consumed a lesser light that I used to love, dimming its brilliance. A flame illuminated me, but that was a flame, and you, divine and lovely, are the crucible of lights; you eclipse her. Because until the sun comes out, a star seems beautiful.

DA. MENCÍA   What a smooth talker! You're very given to poetic conceits.

DON GUTIERRE So, do you mind if I go?

DA. MENCÍA   It's hard to decide. Clearly you want to go.

DON GUTIERRE Can I possibly deceive you, if I take you along in my soul, and my soul stays here with you?

DA. MENCÍA   Well, since you're staying, goodbye, Don Gutierre.

DON GUTIERRE Goodbye.

Don Gutierre leaves. [Jacinta enters.]

JACINTA   Madam, something has left you sad.

DA. MENCÍA   Yes, Jacinta, and with reason.

JACINTA   I don't know what's bothering you; you seem distracted.

DA. MENCÍA   It's true.

535 *Aplico agora*: 'Although *aplicar* is not now used intransitively, Covarrubias … seems to suggest that in this kind of case it was so used. Here it suits the metre better, and is the form found in the first editions' (C. A. Jones in his ed. of Calderón's *El médico de su honra*, p. 20).

JACINTA	Bien puedes fiar de mí.
DOÑA MENCÍA	¿Quieres ver si de ti fío
	mi vida, y el honor mío?
	Pues escucha atenta.
JACINTA	Di.

DOÑA MENCÍA   Nací en Sevilla, y en ella   565
me vio Enrique, festejó
mis desdenes, celebró
mi nombre, ¡felice estrella!
Fuese, y mi padre atropella
la libertad que hubo en mí.   570
La mano a Gutierre di,
volvió Enrique, y en rigor,
tuve amor, y tengo honor:
esto es cuanto sé de mí.

Vanse, y sale doña Leonor, y Inés, con mantos.

INÉS   Ya sale para entrar en la capilla: 575
aquí le espera, y a sus pies te humilla.
DOÑA LEONOR   Lograré mi esperanza,
si recibe mi agravio la venganza.

Sale el Rey, [un Viejo], y Soldados.

[Voz] *(dentro)*	¡Plaza!
[SOLDADO] 1	Tu Majestad aquéste lea.
REY	Yo le haré ver.
[SOLDADO] 2	Tu Alteza, señor, vea 580
	éste.
REY	Está bien.
[SOLDADO] 2	[*Ap.*] Pocas palabras gasta.
[SOLDADO] 3	Yo soy…
REY	El memorial aqueste basta.
[SOLDADO] 3	Turbado estoy; mal el tremor resisto.
REY	¿De qué os turbáis?
[SOLDADO] 3	¿No basta haberos visto?
REY	Sí basta. ¿Qué pedís?
[SOLDADO] 3	Yo soy soldado; 585
	una ventaja.
REY	Poco habéis pedido,
	para haberos turbado:
	una jineta os doy.

JACINTA   Don't worry, you can trust me.

DA. MENCÍA   You want to see if I trust you with my life an[d]
               listen.

JACINTA   Tell me.

DA. MENCÍA   I was born in Seville. Enrique saw me there; ...
               celebrated his love for me. Happy star! He left, and my father
               trampled on my freedom. I gave Gutierre my hand; Enrique
               came back; and this is all I know about myself: once I had love;
               now I have honour.

They leave.

[* *]*

Doña Leonor enters with Inés, both wearing cloaks.

INES   Now he's going into the chapel. Wait for him here, and throw
               yourself at his feet.

DA. LEONOR   My hope will be fulfilled if my grievance is avenged.

Enter the King, [an Old Man], and Soldiers.

[VOICE]   (*Within*) Make way!

FIRST [SOLD.] Your Majesty, please read this.

KING   I'll make certain it's read.

SECOND [SOLD.] Your Highness, sir, please look at this.

KING   Fine.

SECOND [SOLD.] [*Aside*] He doesn't waste any words.

THIRD [SOLD.] I'm –

KING   This document will suffice.

THIRD [SOLD.] I'm shaking in my boots!

KING   What are you afraid of?

THIRD [SOLD.] Isn't it enough just to see you?

KING   Yes, it's enough. What do you want?

THIRD [SOLD.] I'm a soldier – a promotion would be nice.

KING   For being so upset, you ask very little. I promote you to captain
               of the infantry.

---

568 *felice* = *feliz*.

588 *una jineta os doy*: Literally, 'I give you a *jineta*'. A '*jineta*' can be 'a short lance
adorned with a tassel, together with the gilded sword, insignia of captains of the infantry'
(Covarrubias, p. 589b).

⌐LDADO] 3	Felice he sido.
.IEJO	Un pobre viejo soy; limosna os pido.
REY	Tomad este diamante.
VIEJO	¿Para mí os le quitáis?
REY	Y no os espante;

que, para darle de una vez, quisiera
sólo un diamante todo el mundo fuera.

DOÑA LEONOR   Señor, a vuestras plantas
mis pies turbados llegan;
de parte de mi honor vengo a pediros
con voces que se anegan en suspiros,
con suspiros que en lágrimas se anegan,
justicia: para vos y Dios apelo.

REY   Sosegaos, señora, alzad del suelo.

DOÑA LEONOR   Yo soy...

REY   No prosigáis de esa manera.
Salíos todos afuera.

Vanse.

Hablad agora, porque si venisteis
de parte del honor, como dijisteis,
indigna cosa fuera
que en público el honor sus quejas diera,
y que a tan bella cara
vergüenza la justicia le costara.

DOÑA LEONOR   Pedro, a quien llama el mundo Justiciero,
planeta soberano de Castilla,
a cuya luz se alumbra este hemisfero;
Júpiter español, cuya cuchilla
rayos esgrime de templado acero,
cuando blandida al aire alumbra y brilla;
sangriento giro, que entre nubes de oro,
corta los cuellos de uno y otro moro:
  yo soy Leonor, a quien Andalucía
llama (lisonja fue), Leonor la bella;
no porque fuese la hermosura mía
quien el nombre adquirió, sino la estrella;
que quien decía bella, ya decía
infelice, que el nombre incluye y sella,
a la sombra no más de la hermosura,
poca dicha, señor, poca ventura.

Line numbers: 590, 595, 600, 605, 610, 615, 620

THIRD [SOLD.]	What luck!
OLD MAN	I'm a poor old man – can you give me anything?
KING	Take this diamond.
OLD MAN	You give that to me?
KING	Don't be surprised. I wish the whole world were a diamond that I could give you.
DA. LEONOR	Sir, I don't know where else to go – I throw myself at your feet. It's about my honour. I'm begging you through these tears, give me justice! I appeal to you and to God.
KING	Don't go on like that. Everyone else leave.

They go.

Now tell me. If you come as you say about your honour, it would be unwise to discuss your complaint in public, and a pity to cause such a lovely face to blush in shame.

DA. LEONOR   Pedro, known to the world as 'the Enforcer of Justice', sovereign planet of Castile, whose light illuminates this entire hemisphere; Spanish Jupiter, whose blade wields lightning bolts of tempered steel, gleaming and shining as they're brandished in the air; bloody gash that through golden clouds cleaves the throats of many Moors:

I am Leonor. Andalusia calls me 'Leonor the lovely', not for my appearance, but because of my misfortune, since they say that beauty brings unhappiness.

---

609 *el Justiciero*: see 'Historical Contexts and Responses' in Introduction, and the accompanying note 24.

616 **cleaves the throats of many Moors:** This play takes place during the centuries-long Reconquest, when Christian forces were taking back the Iberian Peninsula from the Moors, who had invaded in 711 A.D. The Reconquest finally ended in 1492, with the fall of the last Moorish kingdom, Granada. Prowess in battles against the Moors would be a sign of manliness, glory, and, of course, God's favour.

617 **Andalusia:** The region in southern Spain in which Seville is located.

621–2 *infelice* = *infeliz*. Here Leonor refers to the common belief that beautiful women have bad luck, as expressed in the proverb *la ventura de la fea, la bella la desea* (the beautiful woman wishes for the luck of the ugly one).

Puso los ojos, para darme enojos,   625
un caballero en mí, que ¡ojalá fuera
basilisco de amor a mis despojos,
áspid de celos a mi primavera!
Luego el deseo sucedió a los ojos,
el amor al deseo, y de manera   630
mi calle festejó, que en ella vía
morir la noche, y espirar el día.
    ¿Con qué razones, gran señor, herida
la voz, diré que a tanto amor postrada,
aunque el desdén me publicó ofendida,   635
la voluntad me confesó obligada?
De obligada pasé a agradecida,
luego de agradecida a apasionada;
que en la universidad de enamorados,
dignidades de amor se dan por grados: 640
    poca centella incita mucho fuego,
poco viento movió mucha tormenta,
poca nube al principio arroja luego
mucho diluvio, poca luz alienta
mucho rayo después, poco amor ciego   645
descubre mucho engaño; y así intenta,
siendo centella, viento, nube, ensayo,
ser tormenta, diluvio, incendio y rayo.
    Diome palabra que sería mi esposo;
que éste de las mujeres es el cebo   650
con que engaña el honor el cauteloso
pescador, cuya pasta es el Erebo
que aduerme los sentidos temeroso.
El labio aquí fallece, y no me atrevo
a decir que mintió. No es maravilla.   655
¿Qué palabra se dio para cumplilla?
    Con esta libertad entró en mi casa,
si bien siempre el honor fue reservado;
porque yo, liberal de amor, y escasa

To my misfortune, a gentleman set his eyes on me. Cloaking himself in love, he was a basilisk out to get me; he was a poisonous snake of jealousy! After gazing at me, he began to desire; on the heels of desire was love. He courted me; night and day he haunted the street where I live.

Great sir, how can my trembling voice put this into words? All this love brought me round: although in public I only expressed disdain, secretly my feelings began to change. From interested, I became grateful; from grateful, impassioned; because in the university of lovers, rankings of love are given by degrees:

a small spark ignites a great flame; a little wind stirs a huge storm; a small cloud spawns a great flood; a brief glimmer begets a mighty bolt of lightning; a little blind love leads to much deception. And so my emotion, once a spark, a breeze, a cloud, a glimmer, became a storm, a flood, a conflagration, a bolt of lightning.

He promised to marry me; this is the lure the wily fisherman uses to wreck a woman's honour; his fishing ground is the Erebus that lulls the tender senses, that betrays one's good name.

I can hardly go on. How can I find the courage to tell you that he lied? It's not surprising. What word was ever given to be kept?

With this expectation, he entered my house, although always under honourable circumstances. Because I, liberal with my love, and frugal with my honour, always guarded it well. But

---

627–8 *basilisco de amor a mis despojos, / áspid de celos a mi primavera:* Literally, 'a basilisk of love to my spoils, an asp of jealousy to my springtime'.

652 **Erebus:** In Greek mythology, a dark place in the underworld through which souls pass on their journey to Hades. 'Erebus is not normally associated with drowsiness or forgetfulness, although Calderón here seems to imply that it was' (Jones p. 26).

650–3 *que éste de las mujeres es el cebo / con que engaña el honor el cauteloso / pescador, cuya pasta es el Erebo / que aduerme los sentidos temeroso:* Jones (p. 25) offers the following translation for the passage: 'for this is the bait for women which the cunning fisherman, whose substance is that fearful Erebus which lulls to sleep the senses, uses to deceive honour'.

656 *cumplilla = cumplirla.*

de honor, me atuve siempre a este sagrado.   660
Mas la publicidad a tanto pasa,
y tanto esta opinión se ha dilatado,
que en secreto quisiera más perdella,
que con público escándalo tenella.
    Pedí justicia, pero soy muy pobre;   665
quejéme dél, pero es muy poderoso;
y ya que es imposible que yo cobre,
pues se casó, mi honor, Pedro famoso,
si sobre tu piedad divina, sobre
tu justicia, me admites generoso,   670
que me sustente en un convento pido:
Gutierre Alfonso de Solís ha sido.

REY   Señora, vuestros enojos
siento con razón, por ser
un Atlante en quien descansa   675
todo el peso de la ley.
Si Gutierre está casado,
no podrá satisfacer,
como decís, por entero
vuestro honor; pero yo haré   680
justicia como convenga
en esta parte; si bien
no os debe restituir
honor, que vos os tenéis.
Oigamos a la otra parte   685
disculpas suyas; que es bien
guardar el segundo oído
para quien llega después;
y fiad, Leonor, de mí,
que vuestra causa veré   690
de suerte que no os obligue
a que digáis otra vez
que sois pobre, él poderoso,
siendo yo en Castilla Rey.
Mas Gutierre viene allí;   695
podrá, si conmigo os ve,
conocer que me informasteis
primero. Aquese cancel
os encubra, aquí aguardad,
hasta que salgáis después.   700

rumours began to spread so far that I'd rather have lost my virtue to him in private, than to be the innocent victim of a public scandal.

I asked for justice, but I'm very poor; I lodged a complaint against him, but he's very powerful. And now, it's impossible to restore my good name, because he married someone else.

Renowned Pedro, please be generous, grant my plea: with your divine mercy, with your justice, all I ask is that you make him sponsor me in a convent. It was Gutierre Alfonso de Solís.

KING   Madam, I feel your pain. As King, I'm an Atlas: the entire weight of the law rests on my shoulders. If Gutierre is married, as you say, he won't be able to satisfy your honour completely. Since you never in fact gave up your private honour, you still have that.

But I'll see that justice is done in this matter. Let's hear what the other side has to say, because it's only fair. Trust me, Leonor. As long as I'm King of Castile, I'll make certain that you'll never have to say again that you've suffered because you're poor and he's powerful.

But here comes Gutierre now. If he sees you with me, he'll guess that you've already accused him. Wait behind that screen until afterwards.

---

663   *perdella* = *perderla*: 'la' apparently refers to *opinión*, here meaning Doña Leonor's reputation.

663–4   **I'd rather have lost ... a public scandal**: Leonor explains that although she scrupulously guarded her virginity, her reputation suffered because her suitor frequently visited her home.

671   **sponsor me in a convent**: Women of some social standing and means could withdraw from the world by retiring to a convent, without taking vows. Since they could bring with them the comforts of home, it was not necessarily a very spiritual existence, nor was it inexpensive, but it was a protected life.

675   **Atlas**: In mythology, Atlas was a Titan king who carried the weight of the heavens on his shoulders. See frontispiece.

DOÑA LEONOR   En todo he de obedeceros.

Escóndese, y sale Coquín.

COQUÍN	De sala en sala, pardiez,	
	a la sombra de mi amo,	
	que allí se quedó, llegué	
	hasta aquí, ¡válgame Alá!	705
	¡Vive Dios, que está aquí el Rey!	
	Él me ha visto, y se mesura.	
	¡Plegue al cielo que no esté	
	muy alto aqueste balcón,	
	por si me arroja por él!	710
REY	¿Quién sois?	
COQUÍN	¿Yo, señor?	
REY	Vos.	
COQUÍN	Yo	
	(¡válgame el cielo!) soy quien	
	vuestra Majestad quisiere,	
	sin quitar y sin poner,	
	porque un hombre muy discreto	715
	me dio por consejo ayer,	
	no fuese quien en mi vida	
	vos no quisieseis; y fue	
	de manera la lición,	
	que antes, agora, y después,	720
	quien vos quisiéredes sólo	
	fui, quien gustareis seré,	
	quien os place soy; y en esto,	
	mirad con quién y sin quién…	
	y así, con vuestra licencia,	725
	por donde vine me iré	
	hoy, con mis pies de compás,	
	si no con compás de pies.	

702 *pardiez*: Euphemism for 'por Dios'.
705 *¡valgame Alá!*: Literally, 'Allah save me!'. Wardropper (1970, p. 590) points out that this exclamation was changed in later editions to '¡El cielo me valga!' (Heaven help me!). See 'Coquín' in Introduction, note 16.
708–10 I hope to heaven … chucks me off it!: It is not uncommon in the *comedia* for a character causing displeasure to be thrown off a balcony or out a window. See, for example,

DA. LEONOR   I'll do whatever you command.

She hides, and Coquín enters.

COQUÍN   By golly, I've been following Gutierre around from room to room. He's over there. Praise Allah! Good God, here's the King! He's seen me, and he looks mad. I hope to heaven this balcony isn't very high, just in case he chucks me off it!

KING   Who are you?

COQUÍN   I, sir?

KING   You.

COQUÍN   (Heaven help me!) I'm whoever your Majesty would like, plain and simple, because a very discreet man gave me some advice yesterday. He said never to be anyone you didn't like, and I learned the lesson so well that it went backwards and forwards in time: even before then I made sure to be whoever you wanted; in the future I'll be whoever you could possibly want, and right now I'm exactly the one you like, and as far as this goes, look with whom and without whom … And so, with your permission, I'll just go back the way I came today; off I go, smartly stepping in time to the rhythm in my head.

Act Two of Calderón's *Life Is a Dream* (*La vida es sueño*), where such is the fate of an outspoken servant who angers Prince Segismundo.

719   *lición* = *lección*.

721   *quisiéredes* = *quisiereis*.

722–4 I'll be whoever … without whom …: Coquín 'seems to suggest that the King by now knows only too well with whom he is, and that he is now about to see whom he is without (*sin quien*), since Coquín is about to leave' (Jones, p. 28).

727–8   *con mis pies de compás, / si no con compás de pies:* Literally, 'with my two feet as compass, if not with a pair of compasses'. Here Coquín makes a complex pun with the word *compás*. A **compass** is of course a device that indicates geographical direction; the word also refers to a mathematical instrument with two feet (also called in English 'a pair of compasses'), used for drawing curves and measuring distances. Finally, the expression *de compás* means 'in rhythm' or 'keeping time'; Coquín says he will leave *con mis pies de compás*, which in addition to 'with my [two] feet as compass', means 'keeping time with my feet'.

REY	Aunque me habéis respondido	
	cuanto pudiera saber,	730
	quién sois os he preguntado.	
COQUÍN	Y yo os hubiera también	
	al tenor de la pregunta	
	respondido, a no temer	
	que en diciéndoos quien soy, luego	735
	por un balcón me arrojéis,	
	por haberme entrado aquí	
	tan sin qué ni para qué,	
	teniendo un oficio yo	
	que vos no habéis menester.	740
REY	¿Qué oficio tenéis?	
COQUÍN	Yo soy	
	cierto correo de a pie,	
	portador de todas nuevas,	
	hurón de todo interés,	
	sin que se me haya escapado	745
	señor, profeso o novel;	
	y del que me ha dado más,	
	digo mal, mas digo bien.	
	Todas las casas son mías;	
	y aunque lo son, esta vez	750
	la de don Gutierre Alfonso	
	es mi accesoria, en quien fue	
	mi pasto meridiano,	
	un andaluz cordobés.	
	Soy cofrade del contento;	755
	el pesar no sé quién es,	
	ni aun para servirle: en fin,	
	soy, aquí donde me veis,	
	mayordomo de la risa,	
	gentilhombre del placer	760
	y camarero del gusto,	
	pues que me visto con él.	
	Y por ser esto, he temido	
	el darme aquí a conocer;	
	porque un rey que no se ríe,	765
	temo que me libre cien	
	esportillas batanadas,	
	con pespuntes al envés,	
	por vagamundo.	

KING   You've told me no more than what I could already have guessed.
              I asked you who you are.

COQUÍN   And I'd have answered the question except that if I told you
              who I am, you'd throw me off a balcony for coming in here
              without permission, since I perform a service that you don't
              need at all.

KING   And what's that?

COQUÍN   I'm a sort of postal service on foot. A carrier of all news, a
              ferreter out of anything of interest; nothing high or low escapes
              me, sir; and whoever pays me the most gets the best publicity,
              even if I have to fiddle with the truth. I get into every house,
              although right now I eat my midday meal in the house of don
              Gutierre Alfonso, an Andalusian from Cordoba.

              I'm a member of the National Brotherhood of Clowns. I
              don't know what sadness is; wouldn't recognize it if it smacked
              me in the face. In short, I'm superintendent of laughter; butler
              of delight and chamberlain of chuckles; that is, I dress up in a
              suit of silliness.

              And so I was afraid to tell you in the first place, because a
              king that never laughs will arrest me for idleness and write my
              punishment in lashes on my backside.

750–3   I eat my midday meal ... Don Gutierre Alfonso: In Act Three, lines 2443–4, we
are told that Coquín was raised in Don Gutierre's household.

754   an Andalusian from Cordoba: Jones (p. 29) points out that Coquín may be describing
himself rather than Don Gutierre as an Andalusian from Córdoba. See Introduction, note 16.

**766–8   *temo que me libre cien / esportillas batanadas, / con pespuntes al envés, / por
vagamundo*:** Paraphrased: "'I fear he will deliver to me a hundred baskets (of the sort carried
by *pícaros* for a living) which have been beaten in a fulling mill (*batán*), with knots on
the wrong side (suggesting the beating of a backside with a knotted whip), because I am a
vagrant'" (Wardropper 1970, p. 590).

REY   En fin, ¿sois
                    hombre que a cargo tenéis   770
                    la risa?
COQUÍN   Sí, mi señor;
                    y porque lo echéis de ver,
                    esto es jugar de gracioso
                    en palacio.

Cúbrese.

REY   Está muy bien;
                    y pues sé quién sois, hagamos   775
                    los dos un concierto.
COQUÍN   ¿Y es?
REY   ¿Hacer reír profesáis?
COQUÍN   Es verdad.
REY   Pues cada vez
                    que me hiciéredes reír,
                    cien escudos os daré;   780
                    y si no me hubiereis hecho
                    reír en término de un mes,
                    os han de sacar los dientes.
COQUÍN   Testigo falso me hacéis,
                    y es ilícito contrato   785
                    de inorme lesión.
REY   ¿Por qué?
COQUÍN   Porque quedaré lisiado
                    si le aceto, ¿no se ve?
                    Dicen, cuando uno se ríe,
                    que enseña los dientes; pues   790
                    enseñarlos yo llorando,
                    será reírme al revés.
                    Dicen que sois tan severo,
                    que a todos dientes hacéis;
                    ¿qué os hice yo, que a mí solo   795
                    deshacérmelos queréis?
                    Pero vengo en el partido;
                    que porque ahora me dejéis
                    ir libre, no le rehúso,

KING	In other words, you call yourself a jester?
COQUÍN	Yes, my lord, and just to show you, this is how to perform the part of a jester in a palace.

He puts on his hat.

KING	Very well. And since I now know who you are, let's make a deal.
COQUÍN	Yes?
KING	You claim to make people laugh?
COQUÍN	It's true.
KING	Well, then, every time you make me laugh, I'll give you one hundred gold coins; and if you fail to make me laugh by the end of one month's time, I'll have your teeth pulled out.
COQUÍN	Yikes! You're trying to impugn my profession, and that would be an unlawful contract, with enormous damages.
KING	Why?
COQUÍN	Because I'll wind up enormously damaged if I accept it, don't you see? They say that when a person laughs, he shows his teeth, but when I show them crying, it will be laughing wrong-way-round. They say you're so severe that you show your teeth to everyone, and I don't mean laughing. What did I ever do to you, that you want to undo my teeth?
	But I accept the bargain, just so you'll let me go now. I accept, because it's like finding myself unexpectedly with an

---

772 *porque* = *para que.*

774+ **He puts on his hat:** 'Only grandees (and jesters) had the right to wear their hats in the king's presence' (Cruickshank 1989, p. 110).

784 *Testigo falso me hacéis* can mean 'You'll make me a liar when I claim to be able to make people laugh'; or alternatively, 'You bear false witness against me'.

786 *inorme* = *enorme*. '*Enorme lesión* is a legal term meaning that the buyer has been cheated of more than half the just price. *Lesión* also refers to "bodily harm", as Coquín goes on to explain' (Wardropper 1970, p. 591).

788 *aceto* = *acepto.*

787–8 On the potentially fatal consequences of tooth extraction in Calderón's time, see Ortiz Lottman.

800–2 finding myself unexpectedly: 'To find something in the street' (*hallar una cosa como en la calle*) means 'to find something unexpectedly' (Jones, p. 31).

pues por lo menos un mes   800
me hallo aquí como en la calle
de vida; y al cabo dél,
no es mucho que tome postas
en mi boca la vejez:
y así voy a examinarme   805
de cosquillas. ¡Voto a diez,
que os habéis de reír! Adiós,
y veámonos después.

Vase, y salen don Enrique, don Gutierre, don Diego, y don Arias, y toda la compañía.

DON ENRIQUE   Déme vuestra Majestad
la mano.
REY   Vengáis con bien,   810
Enrique; ¿cómo os sentís?
DON ENRIQUE   Más, señor, el susto fue
que el golpe: estoy bueno.
DON GUTIERRE   A mí
vuestra Majestad me dé
la mano, si mi humildad   815
merece tan alto bien,
porque el suelo que pisáis
es soberano dosel
que ilumina de los vientos
uno y otro rosicler;   820
y vengáis con la salud
que este reino ha menester,
para que os adore España,
coronado de laurel.
REY   De vos, don Gutierre Alfonso…   825
DON GUTIERRE ¿Las espaldas me volvéis?
REY   …grandes querellas me dan.
DON GUTIERRE Injustas deben de ser.
REY   ¿Quién es, decidme, Leonor,
una principal mujer   830
de Sevilla?
DON GUTIERRE   Una señora
bella, ilustre y noble es,
de lo mejor desta tierra.

extra month of life. At the end of the month it won't be so awful if old age puckers up my toothless mouth. So let's test my talent as a tickler. I swear by golly, you're going to laugh! Goodbye, see you later.

He leaves, and the Prince, Don Gutierre, Don Diego, Don Arias, and all their men enter.

PRINCE   Your Majesty, give me your hand.

KING   Welcome, Enrique. How do you feel?

PRINCE   Sir, the shock was greater than the fall. I'm fine.

DON GUTIERRE   Give me your hand, Your Majesty, if such a humble subject deserves such a high honour, because the ground you tread is a supreme dais that illuminates the breezy dawn and dusk. May you enjoy the good health that this realm needs, so that Spain may worship you, crowned with laurel.

KING   As for you, Don Gutierre Alfonso –

DON GUTIERRE   You turn your back on me?

KING   I hear serious complaints.

DON GUTIERRE   They cannot be justified.

KING   Tell me, who is Leonor, a distinguished woman of Seville?

DON GUTIERRE   She's a lovely lady from one of the best families in the land.

803–4 *que tome postas / en mi boca la vejez*: literally, 'should old age take up sentry duty in my mouth'.
806 *Voto a diez*: euphemism for *voto a Dios* (see line 702 note).
817–20 the ground you tread … crowned with laurel: On this passage, Jones writes (p. 32), 'The meaning seems to be that Pedro's throne, symbolizing his royal power, lights up east and west, in other words, all parts of his kingdom. *Rosicler* is normally the rosy glow of dawn, but *uno y otro rosicler* seems to indicate that the glow of sunset is also involved, so that in both east and west, where the sun rises and sets, Pedro's reign gives light'.

REY	¿Qué obligación la tenéis,
	a que habéis correspondido
	necio, ingrato y descortés?
DON GUTIERRE	No os he de mentir en nada,
	que el hombre, señor, de bien
	no sabe mentir jamás,
	y más delante del Rey.
	Servíla, y mi intento entonces
	casarme con ella fue,
	si no mudara las cosas
	de los tiempos el vaivén.
	Visitéla, entré en su casa
	públicamente; si bien
	no le debo a su opinión
	de una mano el interés.
	Viéndome desobligado,
	pude mudarme después;
	y así, libre deste amor,
	en Sevilla me casé
	con doña Mencía de Acuña,
	dama principal, con quien
	vivo, fuera de Sevilla
	una casa de placer.
	Leonor, mal aconsejada
	(que no la aconseja bien
	quien destruye su opinión),
	pleitos intentó poner
	a mi desposorio, donde
	el más riguroso juez
	no halló causa contra mí,
	aunque ella dice que fue
	diligencia del favor.
	¡Mirad vos a qué mujer
	hermosa favor faltara,
	si le hubiera menester!
	Con este engaño pretende,
	puesto que vos lo sabéis,
	valerse de vos; y así,
	yo me pongo a vuestros pies,
	donde a la justicia vuestra
	dará la espada mi fe,

835

840

845

850

855

860

865

870

KING How is it, then, that you've been foolish, ungrateful and discourteous to her?

DON GUTIERRE I won't lie to you about anything, sir, because a good man never lies, especially to his King. I courted her, and at the time I intended to marry her, if things hadn't changed.

I visited her publicly at her home, although not compromising her reputation to the extent that I would have had to give her my hand in marriage. Seeing that I owed her nothing, I changed my mind. And so, breaking off this relationship, in Seville I married Doña Mencía de Acuña, a prominent lady with whom I live outside the city in a country home.

Leonor, following bad advice (because advice that destroys one's reputation is badly given) sued me for breach of promise, but even the strictest judge found for me, although she claims it was because of favouritism. Look, what beautiful woman ever lacked favour if she needed it?

Since you already know about it, she must be trying to gain your support. And so I loyally throw myself at your feet, where you can bring your sword down upon my head.

	y mi lealtad la cabeza.	875
REY	¿Qué causa tuvisteis, pues,	
	para tan grande mudanza?	
DON GUTIERRE	¿Novedad tan grande es	
	mudarse un hombre? ¿No es cosa	
	que cada día se ve?	880
REY	Sí; pero de extremo a extremo	
	pasar el que quiso bien,	
	no fue sin grande ocasión.	
DON GUTIERRE	Suplícoos no me apretéis;	
	que soy hombre que, en ausencia	885
	de las mujeres, daré	
	la vida por no decir	
	cosa indigna de su ser.	
REY	¿Luego vos causa tuvisteis?	
DON GUTIERRE	Sí, señor; pero creed	890
	que si para mi descargo	
	hoy hubiera menester	
	decirlo, cuando importara	
	vida y alma, amante fiel	
	de su honor, no lo dijera.	895
REY	Pues yo lo quiero saber.	
DON GUTIERRE	Señor…	
REY	Es curiosidad.	
DON GUTIERRE	Mirad…	
REY	No me repliquéis;	
	que me enojaré, por vida…	
DON GUTIERRE	Señor, señor, no juréis;	900
	que menos importa mucho	
	que yo deje aquí de ser	
	quien soy, que veros airado.	
REY	([*Ap.*] Que dijese le apuré	
	el suceso en alta voz,	905
	porque pueda responder	
	Leonor, si aquéste me engaña;	
	y si habla verdad, porque,	
	convencida con su culpa,	
	sepa Leonor que lo sé.)	910
	Decid, pues.	
DON GUTIERRE	A mi pesar	
	lo digo: una noche entré	

KING	Well, why did you have such a major change of heart?
DON GUTIERRE	Is it so unusual for a man to change his mind? Doesn't it happen every day?
KING	Yes, but for a man who truly loved to go from one extreme to the other, there must have been a good reason.
DON GUTIERRE	I beg you not to press me on this. I'm a man who would die before saying anything behind a woman's back that might damage her reputation.
KING	So you did have a good reason?
DON GUTIERRE	Yes, sir. But please believe that if I had to tell you in order to exonerate myself, even if my life and soul depended on it, I wouldn't tell you – because I'm faithful to her good name.
KING	Well, I want to know.
DON GUTIERRE	Sir –
KING	Out of curiosity.
DON GUTIERRE	Look –
KING	Don't talk back to me, because if I get angry, for the life of –
DON GUTIERRE	Sir, sir, don't swear! It's much better for me to fail in my duty as a gentleman than to see your wrath.
KING	([*Aside*] I'm forcing him to say what happened out loud, so that Leonor can respond, in case he's lying to me. And if he speaks the truth, so that Leonor, unable to deny her guilt, will know that I know.) Then tell me.
DON GUTIERRE	I'll tell you, reluctantly: one night I went into her house, I heard

---

902–3 *que yo deje aquí de ser / quien soy*: Literally, 'that here I leave off being who I am'. See line 133 note on the phrase S*oy quien soy*.

	en su casa, sentí ruido	
	en una cuadra, llegué,	
	y al mismo tiempo que ya	915
	fui a entrar, pude el bulto ver	
	de un hombre, que se arrojó	
	del balcón; bajé tras él,	
	y sin conocerle, al fin	
	pudo escaparse por pies.	920

DON ARIAS   [*Ap.*] ¡Válgame el cielo! ¿Qué es esto
                 que miro?

DON GUTIERRE   Y aunque escuché
                 satisfacciones, y nunca
                 di a mi agravio entera fe,
                 fue bastante esta aprehensión   925
                 a no casarme; porque
                 si amor y honor son pasiones
                 del ánimo, a mi entender,
                 quien hizo al amor ofensa,
                 se la hace al honor en él;   930
                 porque el agravio del gusto
                 al alma toca también.

Sale doña Leonor.

DOÑA LEONOR   Vuestra Majestad perdone;
                 que no puedo detener
                 el golpe a tantas desdichas   935
                 que han llegado de tropel.

REY   [*Ap.*] ¡Vive Dios, que me engañaba!
                 La prueba sucedió bien.

DOÑA LEONOR   Y oyendo contra mi honor
                 presunciones, fuera ley   940
                 injusta que yo, cobarde,
                 dejara de responder;
                 que menos perder importa
                 la vida, cuando me dé
                 este atrevimiento muerte,   945
                 que vida y honor perder.
                 Don Arias entró en mi casa…

DON ARIAS   Señora, espera, detén
                 la voz. Vuestra Majestad,
                 licencia, señor, me dé,   950

a noise in a room, and as I entered it, I could see the shape of a man jumping off the balcony. I went down after him, and he escaped on foot before I could see who it was.

DON ARIAS   [*Aside*] Good heavens! What's this I see?

DON GUTIERRE   And although I listened to her explanations, and I was never really sure I'd been wronged, it was enough not to marry her. Because if love and honour are passions of the spirit, I believe that one who offends love, also offends honour. If feelings are wronged, it also touches one's soul.

Doña Leonor enters.

DA. LEONOR   Forgive me, Your Majesty, but I must defend myself against all these misrepresentations.

KING   [*Aside*] By God, he was deceiving me! My test worked.

DA. LEONOR   And hearing so many insults to my honour, I couldn't let fear keep me from responding: I'd rather lose my life, if this audacity brings me death, than lose both my life and my honour. Don Arias came into my house –

DON ARIAS   Wait, Madam, don't go on. Your Majesty, sir, please allow me to speak, because it's my duty to defend this lady's honour.

921–2 What's this I see?: A repetition of line 82. In this case it is what is *heard*, rather than seen, that is being remarked upon. A similar transposition of these two senses occurs in line 2176. See Blue.

porque el honor desta dama
me toca a mí defender.
Esa noche estaba en casa
de Leonor una mujer
con quien me hubiera casado,   955
si de la parca el cruel
golpe no cortara fiera
su vida. Yo, amante fiel
de su hermosura, seguí
sus pasos, y en casa entré   960
de Leonor (atrevimiento
de enamorado) sin ser
parte a estorbarlo Leonor.
Llegó don Gutierre, pues;
temerosa, Leonor dijo   965
que me retirase a aquel
aposento; yo lo hice.
¡Mil veces mal haya, amén,
quien de una mujer se rinde
a admitir el parecer!   970
Sintióme, entró, y a la voz
de marido, me arrojé
por el balcón; y si entonces
volví el rostro a su poder
porque era marido, hoy,   975
que dice que no lo es,
vuelvo a ponerme delante.
Vuestra Majestad me dé
campo en que defienda altivo
que no he faltado a quien es   980
Leonor, pues a un caballero
se le concede la ley.
DON GUTIERRE Yo saldré donde…

[Empuñan.]

REY   ¿Qué es esto?
¿Cómo las manos tenéis
en las espadas delante   985
de mí? ¿No tembláis de ver
mi semblante? Donde estoy,
¿hay soberbia ni altivez?

That night a woman was in Leonor's house that I would have married, if cruel death hadn't cut her life short. I was in love with the beautiful lady. With a lover's boldness, I followed her into Leonor's house, and Leonor couldn't stop me. Then Don Gutierre arrived. Leonor was worried, and she told me to go into that room, so I did.

A thousand curses on the man who follows a woman's advice, amen! He heard me; he came in; and when I heard the husband's voice, I jumped from the balcony. And although at the time I fled from him because I thought he had the authority of a husband, today, since he says he doesn't, I step forward.

Your Majesty, please allow me to defend Leonor's good name on the field – the law allows gentlemen to duel.

DON GUTIERRE   I'll tell you where you can go –

[*They grasp their swords.*]

KING   What's this? You dare lay your hands on your swords in my presence? Don't you tremble to see my face? Where I am, can there be such arrogance? Arrest them at once, and keep them in two

---

980–1 *quien es / Leonor* / **Leonor's reputation**, but literally, 'who Leonor is', once again recalling the phrase *Soy quien soy*. See line 133 note.

982   *le* = *lo*: The field (*el campo* of line 979); that is, where a duel can take place.

983–6   **You dare lay your hands on your swords in my presence?:** Baring a weapon in the presence of the king constituted *lèse majesté*, or extreme disrespect of the royal person. *Lèse majesté* was a very serious offense, punishable by death.

           en dos torres los tened;   990
           y agradeced que no os pongo
           las cabezas a los pies.

Vase.

DON ARIAS   Si perdió Leonor por mí
           su opinión, por mí también
           la tendrá; que esto se debe   995
           al honor de una mujer.

Vase.

DON GUTIERRE [*Ap.*] No siento en desdicha tal
           ver riguroso y cruel
           al Rey; sólo siento que hoy,
           Mencía, no te he de ver.   1000

Vase.

DON ENRIQUE   (*[Ap.]* Con ocasión de la caza,
           preso Gutierre, podré
           ver esta tarde a Mencía.)
           Don Diego, conmigo ven;
           que tengo de porfiar   1005
           hasta morir, o vencer.

Vanse.

DOÑA LEONOR ¡Muerta quedo! ¡Plegue a Dios,
           ingrato, aleve y cruel,
           falso, engañador, fingido,
           sin fe, sin Dios y sin ley,   1010
           que como inocente pierdo
           mi honor, venganza me dé
           el cielo! ¡El mismo dolor
           sientas que siento, y a ver
           llegues, bañado en tu sangre,   1015
           deshonras tuyas, porque
           mueras con las mismas armas
           que matas, amén, amén!
           ¡Ay de mí!, mi honor perdí;
           ¡ay de mí!, mi muerte hallé.   1020

Vase.

towers. Just be grateful that I don't lay your heads at your feet.

He leaves.

DON ARIAS   If Leonor lost her reputation because of me, because of me she'll have it back. It's the least I can do for a woman's honour.

He leaves.

DON GUTIERRE [*Aside.*] I don't regret seeing the King so angry and cruel in this misfortune, as much as I regret that today, Mencía, I won't see you.

He leaves.

PRINCE   ([*Aside.*] With Gutierre under arrest, and on the pretext of hunting, this evening I'll be able to see Mencía.) Don Diego, come with me; I'm going to persevere until death, or victory.

They leave.

DA. LEONOR   I'm dead! You ingrate, treacherous and cruel; liar, deceitful and dishonest; faithless, godless criminal, who caused me, an innocent, to lose my honour – may heaven avenge me! May you feel the same pain that I feel, and may you come to see your own dishonours, bathed in your blood; may you die by the same weapons that you use to kill, amen, amen! Alas, I lost my honour! Alas, I've met my death!

She leaves.

SEGUNDA JORNADA

Salen Jacinta y don Enrique como a escuras.

JACINTA	Llega con silencio.
DON ENRIQUE	Apenas
	los pies en la tierra puse.
JACINTA	Éste es el jardín, y aquí,
	pues de la noche te encubre
	el manto, y pues don Gutierre 1025
	está preso, no hay que dudes
	sino que conseguirás
	vitorias de amor tan dulces.
DON ENRIQUE	Si la libertad, Jacinta,
	que te prometí, presumes 1030
	poco premio a bien tan grande,
	pide más, y no te excuses
	por cortedad: vida y alma
	es bien que por tuyas juzgues.
JACINTA	Aquí mi señora siempre 1035
	viene, y tiene por costumbre
	pasar un poco la noche.
DON ENRIQUE	Calla, calla, no pronuncies
	otra razón, porque temo
	que los vientos nos escuchen. 1040
JACINTA	Ya, pues, porque tanta ausencia
	no me indicie, o no me culpe
	deste delito, no quiero
	faltar de allí.

Vase.

DON ENRIQUE	Amor ayude
	mi intento. Estas verdes hojas 1045
	me escondan y disimulen;
	que no seré yo el primero
	que a vuestras espaldas hurte
	rayos al sol: Acteón
	con Diana me disculpe. 1050

Escóndese, y sale doña Mencía y criadas.

ACT TWO

Jacinta and the Prince enter, as if in the dark.

JACINTA	Come quietly.
PRINCE	My feet are hardly touching the ground.
JACINTA	This is the garden. Here, under the cloak of darkness, and with Gutierre imprisoned, your love will win the sweetest victories.
PRINCE	Jacinta, if the freedom I promised you seems too little reward for arranging this for me, just ask for anything – my life and soul are yours.
JACINTA	My mistress always comes here and spends a little of the evening.
PRINCE	Sh, sh, don't say anything more: I'm afraid the winds might overhear us.
JACINTA	I must go back, or they'll notice I'm gone, and I'll be in trouble for doing this.

She goes.

PRINCE	Love, smooth my path. Green leaves, hide me – I won't be the first man who steals the sun's rays from behind your cover: Actaeon's example with Diana proves it.

He hides. Doña Mencía and her maids enter.

1020+ *como a escuras* = *oscuras*: Because Golden Age *comedias* were performed in the open air during daylight hours, actors conveyed the time of day with dialogue, gestures, movements, dress, etc. See Introduction, on 'Staging and Setting'.

1028 *vitorias* = *victorias*.

1039-40 the winds might overhear us: For a seminal discussion of Calderón's affinity for the cosmic elements, see E. M. Wilson (1936). Wardropper (1958, p.10) notes that air is the dominant element in this play.

1049–50 Actaeon's example with Diana proves it: The story is told in Ovid's *Metamorphoses* III, 138-52. As Diana – goddess of chastity, the moon, and the hunt – bathed in a secluded pool, attended by her nymphs, the hunter Actaeon came upon the scene. Although Enrique has already foreshadowed his identification with this figure in lines 273-4, here he appears to forget the rest of the story: that the angry goddess changed Actaeon into a stag, and his own hounds, not recognizing him, tore him to pieces. See Fox 2001.

DOÑA MENCÍA   ¡Silvia, Jacinta, Teodora!
JACINTA   ¿Qué mandas?
DOÑA MENCÍA   Que traigas luces;
               y venid todas conmigo
               a divertir pesadumbres
               de la ausencia de Gutierre,   1055
               donde el natural presume
               vencer hermosos países
               que el arte dibuja y pule.
               ¡Teodora!
TEODORA   Señora mía.
DOÑA MENCÍA   Divierte con voces dulces   1060
               esta tristeza.
TEODORA   Holgaréme
               que de letra y tono gustes.

Canta Teodora, y duérmese doña Mencía.

JACINTA   No cantes más, que parece
               que ya el sueño al alma infunde
               sosiego y descanso; y pues   1065
               hallaron sus inquietudes
               en él sagrado, nosotras
               no la despertemos.
TEODORA   Huye
               con silencio la ocasión.
JACINTA   [*Ap.*] Yo lo haré, porque la busque   1070
               quien la deseó. ¡O criadas,
               y cuántas honras ilustres
               se han perdido por vosotras!

Vanse, y sale don Enrique.

DON ENRIQUE   Sola se quedó. No duden
               mis sentidos tanta dicha,   1075
               y ya que a esto me dispuse,
               pues la ventura me falta,
               tiempo y lugar me aseguren.
                   ¡Hermosísima Mencía!
DOÑA MENCÍA   ¡Válgame Dios!

Despierta.

DON ENRIQUE   No te asustes.   1080

DA. MENCÍA	Silvia, Jacinta, Teodora!
JACINTA	Yes, Madam?
DA. MENCÍA	Bring lights, and help me forget my unhappiness over Gutierre's absence. Come with me to this lovely spot, where nature surpasses any landscape artist. Teodora!
TEODORA	Madam.
DA. MENCÍA	Sing a sweet song to help me get over my sadness.
TEODORA	I hope you like the words and the tune.

Teodora sings, and Doña Mencía sleeps.

JACINTA	Stop singing: it looks as if she's sleeping now. She's found refuge from her worries; let's not wake her.
TEODORA	Yes, we'll go quietly.
JACINTA	[*Aside*] I certainly will, so that her pursuer may find her. Oh, maidservants, how many glorious reputations have you helped to ruin!

They leave, and Don Enrique enters.

PRINCE	She's alone now. I can hardly believe I have this chance. Now that I've made up my mind to go ahead, this is the time and the place to compensate for my bad luck. Dearest, loveliest Mencía!
DA. MENCÍA	God help me!

She awakens.

PRINCE	Don't be afraid.

DOÑA MENCÍA	¿Qué es esto?
DON ENRIQUE	Un atrevimiento,
	a quien es bien que disculpen
	tantos años de esperanza.
DOÑA MENCÍA	¿Pues, señor, vos…
DON ENRIQUE	No te turbes.
DOÑA MENCÍA	…desta suerte…
DON ENRIQUE	No te alteres.
DOÑA MENCÍA	…entrasteis…
DON ENRIQUE	No te disgustes.
DOÑA MENCÍA	…en mi casa sin temer
	que así a una mujer destruye,
	y que así ofende un vasallo
	tan generoso y ilustre?
DON ENRIQUE	Esto es tomar tu consejo.
	Tú me aconsejas que escuche
	disculpas de aquella dama,
	y vengo a que te disculpes
	conmigo de mis agravios.
DOÑA MENCÍA	Es verdad, la culpa tuve;
	pero si he de disculparme,
	tu Alteza, señor, no dude
	que es en orden a mi honor.
DON ENRIQUE	¿Que ignoro, acaso presumes,
	el respeto que les debo
	a tu sangre y tus costumbres?
	El achaque de la caza,
	que en estos campos dispuse,
	no fue fatigar la caza,
	estorbando que saluden
	a la venida del día,
	sino a ti, garza, que subes
	tan remontada, que tocas
	por las campañas azules
	de los palacios del sol
	los dorados balaústres.

1085

1090

1095

1100

1105

1110

DA. MENCÍA	What's this?
PRINCE	I've waited so long for this, you'll understand why I'm so bold.
DA. MENCÍA	Sir, you – ?
PRINCE	Don't be upset.
DA. MENCÍA	– you came in –
PRINCE	Settle down.
DA. MENCÍA	– like this –
PRINCE	Don't be angry.
DA. MENCÍA	– into my house, without considering that you could destroy me, and that you offend such a noble and illustrious vassal?
PRINCE	I'm just following your advice. You suggested that I should listen to the lady's explanation, and here I am. Tell me what happened.
DA. MENCÍA	You're right, it's my fault, but if I'm going to explain myself, Your Highness, you can be sure that it will only prove my honour.
PRINCE	Perhaps you think I ignore the respect your blood and your virtue deserve? The purpose of the hunt that I arranged in these parts wasn't to chase and kill the game, but to come after you, my heron, you who soar so high through the azure fields that you touch the golden balustrades of the palaces of the sun.

1080–6 God help me! ... into my house: Characters' alternating partial lines 'to form one metrically correct line, thereby preserving the meter amid rapid dialogue', is called stichomythia, and is a common stylistic feature of Calderón's writing. Often the effect of this kind of exchange is to convey a dramatic sense of urgency, as the characters' lines when actually spoken cut each other off. It is a venerable stylistic recourse, dating back at least to Sophocles. See *The New Princeton Encyclopedia of Poetry and Poetics*, p. 1214a. See also Act I, lines 897–8.

1090 *generoso*: See line 291 note.

1103–12 The purpose of the hunt ... palaces of the sun: Frequently in the *comedia*, as in the medieval ballad tradition, a character who hunts is symbolically seeking an amorous encounter. On the 'love-hunt', see Edith Randam Rogers, pp. 15–20. Wardropper (1970, p. 593) also notes that 'the imagery of love-making as a heron hunt is common in lyric poetry'. Citing Alfonso Reyes (*Capítulos de literatura española: segunda serie* [México 1945], pp. 91–99), he writes that 'the Heron is *altiva*, "high-flying", "proud", "disdainful", a great challenge to the lover-huntsman'.

DOÑA MENCÍA	Muy bien, señor, vuestra Alteza	
	a las garzas atribuye	
	esta lucha; pues la garza	1115
	de tal instinto presume,	
	que volando hasta los cielos,	
	rayo de pluma sin lumbre,	
	ave de fuego con alma,	
	con instinto alada nube,	1120
	parda cometa sin fuego,	
	quiere que su intento burlen	
	azores reales; y aun dicen	
	que cuando de todos huye,	
	conoce el que ha de matarla;	1125
	y así, antes que con él luche,	
	el temor hace que tiemble,	
	se estremezca, y se espeluce.	
	Así yo, viendo a tu alteza,	
	quedé muda, absorta estuve,	1130
	conocí el riesgo, y temblé;	
	tuve miedo, y horror tuve:	
	porque mi temor no ignore,	
	porque mi espanto no dude,	
	que es quien me ha de dar la muerte.	1135
DON ENRIQUE	Ya llegué a hablarte, ya tuve	
	ocasión; no he de perdella.	
DOÑA MENCÍA	¿Cómo esto los cielos sufren?	
	Daré voces.	
DON ENRIQUE	A ti misma	
	te infamas.	
DOÑA MENCÍA	¿Cómo no acuden	1140
	a darme favor las fieras?	
DON ENRIQUE	Porque de enojarme huyen.	

Dentro don Gutierre.

DON GUTIERRE	Ten ese estribo, Coquín,	
	y llama a esa puerta.	
DOÑA MENCÍA	¡Cielos!	
	No mintieron mis recelos;	1145
	llegó de mi vida el fin.	
	Don Gutierre es éste, ¡ay Dios!	
DON ENRIQUE	¡O qué infelice nací!	

DA. MENCÍA	Your Highness is right to attribute such flight to the heron, sir, because the heron flies up to the heavens. She has so much heart, she's a russet plume of lightning; a fiery bird with a soul; a winged cloud with a spirit; a dark, fireless comet as she tries to escape the hunt of the royal hawks. They even say that when she flies from them, she knows which one is going to kill her; and so, before she fights against him, fear makes her tremble; she shudders; and she's filled with dread. Just as when I saw Your Highness, I was struck dumb, I was transfixed, I recognized the danger, and I trembled; I was afraid; I was horrified: because my shock and my fear tell me that I've met the one who is going to cause my death.
PRINCE	I had the chance and I'm not going to lose it: I've come to speak with you.
DA. MENCÍA	How can the heavens allow this to happen? I'll scream.
PRINCE	That will only dishonour you.
DA. MENCÍA	Why is this happening?
PRINCE	Because I'm the prince, and I want it.

Don Gutierre, outside.

DON GUTIERRE	Hold that stirrup, Coquín, and knock on the door.
DA. MENCÍA	Good heavens! My fears are coming true; I'm finished. Oh, God, it's Don Gutierrre.
PRINCE	Why am I so unlucky?

1125   when she flies from them … will kill her: Cruickshank (1989, p. 128) points out that it was commonly held that the heron could tell which hunting bird would bring it down. **1140–1   *¿Cómo no acuden / a darme favor las fieras?*** Literally, 'why don't the wild beasts come to help me?'

DOÑA MENCÍA	¿Qué ha de ser, señor, de mí,
	si os halla conmigo a vos? 1150
DON ENRIQUE	¿Pues qué he de hacer?
DOÑA MENCÍA	Retiraros.
DON ENRIQUE	¿Yo me tengo de esconder?
DOÑA MENCÍA	El honor de una mujer
	a más que esto ha de obligaros.
	No podéis salir (¡soy muerta!), 1155
	que como allá no sabían
	mis criadas lo que hacían,
	abrieron luego la puerta.
	Aun salir no podéis ya.
DON ENRIQUE	¿Qué haré en tanta confusión? 1160
DOÑA MENCÍA	Detrás de ese pabellón,
	que en mi misma cuadra está,
	os esconded.
DON ENRIQUE	No he sabido,
	hasta la ocasión presente,
	qué es temor. ¡O qué valiente 1165
	debe de ser un marido!

Escóndese.

DOÑA MENCÍA	Si, inocente la mujer,
	no hay desdicha que no aguarde,
	¡válgame Dios, qué cobarde
	culpada debe de ser! 1170

Salen don Gutierre y Coquín.

DON GUTIERRE	Mi bien, señora, los brazos
	darme una y mil veces puedes.
DOÑA MENCÍA	Con envidia destas redes,
	que en tan amorosos lazos
	están inventando abrazos. 1175
DON GUTIERRE	No dirás que no he venido
	a verte.
DOÑA MENCÍA	Fineza ha sido
	de amante firme y constante.
DON GUTIERRE	No dejo de ser amante
	yo, mi bien, por ser marido; 1180
	que por propia la hermosura
	no desmerece jamás

DA. MENCÍA	Sir, what's going to happen to me if he finds you here?
PRINCE	Well, what should I do?
DA. MENCÍA	Get out of here.
PRINCE	I have to hide?
DA. MENCÍA	A woman's honour should compel you to do more than that. You can't leave now. Since my servants didn't know about you, they opened the door for him. You can't even get out now. I'm dead!
PRINCE	I'm so confused – what can I do?
DA. MENCÍA	Hide behind the canopy in my bedroom.
PRINCE	I never knew fear until now. Oh, a husband must be so brave!

He hides.

DA. MENCÍA	If an innocent woman has so much to fear, good God, how awful must it be for the guilty one!

Don Gutierre and Coquín enter.

DON GUTIERRE	My dear lady, come hold me.
DA. MENCÍA	I will, like vines that lovingly cling to a trellis.
DON GUTIERRE	Now you can't complain that I haven't come to see you.
DA. MENCÍA	It's exactly what one would expect of an unswerving and constant lover.
DON GUTIERRE	Just because I'm your husband doesn't mean I'm not your lover anymore. And besides, beauty in and of itself always deserves

---

1173–5 *estas redes ... están inventando abrazos*: literally, 'these nets, that fashion embraces in such loving ties'. Nets, like trellises, were used to support some plants that intertwined with them.

las finezas; antes más
las alienta y asegura:
y así a su riesgo procura   1185
los medios, las ocasiones.
DOÑA MENCÍA   En obligación me pones.
DON GUTIERRE El alcaide que conmigo
está, es mi deudo y amigo,
y quitándome prisiones   1190
   al cuerpo, más las echó
al alma, porque me ha dado
ocasión de haber llegado
a tan grande dicha yo,
como es a verte.
DOÑA MENCÍA   ¿Quién vio   1195
mayor gloria…
DON GUTIERRE   …que la mía?;
aunque, si bien advertía,
hizo muy poco por mí
en dejarme que hasta aquí
viniese; pues si vivía   1200
   yo sin alma en la prisión,
por estar en ti, mi bien,
darme libertad fue bien,
para que en esta ocasión
alma y vida con razón   1205
otra vez se viese unida;
porque estaba dividida,
teniendo en prolija calma,
en una prisión el alma,
y en otra prisión la vida.   1210
DOÑA MENCÍA   Dicen que dos instrumentos
conformemente templados,
por los ecos dilatados
comunican los acentos:
toca el uno, y los vientos   1215
hiere el otro, sin que allí
nadie le toque; y en mí
esta experiencia se viera;
pues si el golpe allá te hiriera,
muriera yo desde aquí.   1220

admiration. In fact, it commands admiration, and so it creates the means and the opportunities.

DA. MENCÍA   I'm grateful.

DON GUTIERRE The warden in the tower is a relative and a friend of mine. When he freed me, he forever won my gratitude, because he's given me the most wonderful opportunity: the chance to see you.

DA. MENCÍA   When has there ever been such good luck –

DON GUTIERRE – as mine? Although the warden considered his gesture small, if he even thought about it at all, in allowing me to come here. But, my dear, he's permitted my soul, separated from my life, to join together into one now: in prison I lived without my soul, because it was here with you. I'd been divided, my soul tediously becalmed in one prison, and my life in another.

DA. MENCÍA   They say that two stringed instruments, when perfectly in tune, transmit the tones by echoing each other: play the one, and the other, though untouched, is moved by the whisper of the wind. And so it is with me: if a blow struck you there, I would die here.

1208 *calma* can be a nautical term: 'It means stillness of the wind. To be becalmed, to be unable to do anything; like the ship that with the calm is stationary' (Covarrubias, p. 237).

COQUÍN	¿Y no le darás, señora,
	tu mano por un momento
	a un preso de cumplimiento;
	pues llora, siente y ignora
	por qué siente, y por qué llora 1225
	y está su muerte esperando
	sin saber por qué, ni cuándo?
	Pero…
DOÑA MENCÍA	Coquín, ¿qué hay en fin?
COQUÍN	Fin al principio en Coquín
	hay, que esto te estoy contando: 1230
	mucho el Rey me quiere, pero
	si el rigor pasa adelante,
	mi amo será muerto andante,
	pues irá con escudero.
DOÑA MENCÍA	[*a don Gutierre*] Poco regalarte espero; 1235
	porque como no aguardaba
	huésped, descuidada estaba.
	Cena os quiero apercibir.
DON GUTIERRE	Una esclava puede ir.
DOÑA MENCÍA	¿Ya, señor, no va una esclava? 1240
	Yo lo soy, y lo he de ser.
	Jacinta, venme a ayudar.
	([*Ap.*] En salud me he de curar.
	Ved, honor, cómo ha de ser,
	porque me he de resolver 1245
	a una temeraria acción.)

Vanse los dos.

DON GUTIERRE	Tú, Coquín, a esta ocasión
	aquí te queda, y extremos
	olvida, y mira que habemos
	de volver a la prisión 1250
	antes del día; ya falta
	poco; aquí puedes quedarte.
COQUÍN	Yo quisiera aconsejarte
	una industria, la más alta
	que el ingenio humano esmalta: 1255
	en ella tu vida está.
	¡O qué industria…
DON GUTIERRE	Dila ya.

COQUÍN	And madam, won't you give your hand t̶
	honorary prisoner? Because I wail and ṣ
	slightest idea why or when. But –
DA. MENCÍA	Yes, Coquín, what is it?
COQUÍN	It's the beginning of the end of Coquín, let
	King loves me a lot, but if he gets any stricte̲, ..ṣy master will
	be a corpse-errant, because he'll be accompanied by a dead
	squire.
DA. MENCÍA	[*to Don Gutierre*] I can't offer you much, because I wasn't
	expecting anyone. I'll get you some supper.
DON GUTIERRE	A slave woman can do that.
DA. MENCÍA	Aren't I your slave? I'll do it. Jacinta, come with me to help.
	([*Aside*] I've got to cure this disease before it strikes. Honour,
	this is how it must be: I've made up my mind to take a dangerous
	risk.)

The two women leave.

DON GUTIERRE	Coquín, you stay here now, and don't do anything stupid.
	Remember, we've got to go back to the prison before daybreak.
	It's almost time. You stay here.
COQUÍN	I'd like to make a suggestion. Perhaps the best one that a human
	brain can think of. Your life depends on it. Oh, what a great
	plan –
DON GUTIERRE	So tell me.

1242 Jacinta, come with me to help: Although there is no direction to indicate at what point Jacinta has come on stage, one could speculate that she enters now, in response to Mencía's summons.

1243 I've got to cure this disease before it strikes: Curing a malady before it has overcome the patient can be considered a sub-motif of *The Physician*, and Coquín's advice that follows, to stay out of prison 'safe and sound' (1259), extends the theme. See also lines 1467 and 2392–3.

1249 *habemos* = *hemos.*

1254 *industria*: 'It is the skill, diligence, and industry with which one does anything with less work than another' (Covarrubias, p. 666b).

[QUÍN]	…para salir sin lisión,
	sano y bueno de prisión!
DON GUTIERRE	¿Cuál es?
COQUÍN	No volver allá.
	¿No estás bueno? ¿No estás sano?
	Con no volver, claro ha sido
	que sano y bueno has salido.
DON GUTIERRE	¡Vive Dios, necio, villano,
	que te mate por mi mano!
	¿Pues tú me has de aconsejar
	tan vil acción, sin mirar
	la confianza que aquí
	hizo el alcaide de mí?
COQUÍN	Señor, yo llego a dudar
	(que soy más desconfiado)
	de la condición del Rey;
	y así, el honor de esa ley
	no se entiende en el criado;
	y hoy estoy determinado
	a dejarte y no volver.
DON GUTIERRE	¿Dejarme tú?
COQUÍN	¿Qué he de hacer?
DON GUTIERRE	Y de ti ¿qué han de decir?
COQUÍN	Y ¿heme de dejar morir
	por sólo bien parecer?
	Si el morir, señor, tuviera
	descarte o enmienda alguna,
	cosa que de dos la una
	un hombre hacerla pudiera,
	yo probara la primera
	por servirte; mas ¿no ves
	que rifa la vida es?
	Entro en ella, vengo y tomo
	cartas, y piérdola: ¿cómo
	me desquitaré después?
	Perdida se quedará,
	si la pierdo por tu engaño,
	hasta, hasta ciento y un año.

1260

1265

1270

1275

1280

1285

1290

Sale doña Mencía sola, muy alborotada.

DOÑA MENCÍA Señor, tu favor me da.

[COQUÍN]	– to get out of prison, safe and sound!
DON GUTIERRE	What is it?
COQUÍN	Don't go back. Aren't you safe and sound now? If you don't go back, obviously, you've gotten out safe and sound.
DON GUTIERRE	My God, you fool, you villain, I could kill you with my own hands! You're telling me to do something so vile, without considering that the warden trusted me?
COQUÍN	Sir, I'm beginning to have doubts (because I'm a very dubious character) about the King. It seems to me that this scruple of yours for the sake of honour doesn't apply to the servant, so today I've made up my mind to leave you and never come back.
DON GUTIERRE	You'd leave me?
COQUÍN	Well, what should I do?
DON GUTIERRE	And what would everyone say about you then?
COQUÍN	So should I give up my life just for the sake of what people say? Sir, if death had a cure, or supposing one could simply toss it away, I would do so in order to continue serving you, but don't you see that life is like a game of chance? I enter the game, I draw my cards, and I lose it: how can I undo that afterwards? If I lose my life because of your folly, it will stay lost, for – for a hundred and one years.

Doña Mencía enters alone, very upset.

DA. MENCÍA	Sir, I need your help.

1283   *cosa que*: 'What if', 'supposing', a phrase also occurring in line 2388. See Victor Dixon's note to line 2835 on *cosa que* in his edition of Lope de Vega, *El perro del hortelano*.

DON GUTIERRE	¡Válgame Dios! ¿Qué será?	1295
	¿Qué puede haber sucedido?	
DOÑA MENCÍA	Un hombre…	
DON GUTIERRE	¡Presto!	
DOÑA MENCÍA	…escondido	

en mi aposento he topado,
encubierto y rebozado.
Favor, Gutierre, te pido.   1300

DON GUTIERRE   ¿Qué dices? ¡Válgame el cielo!
Ya es forzoso que me asombre.
¿Embozado en casa un hombre?

DOÑA MENCÍA   Yo le vi.

DON GUTIERRE   Todo soy hielo.
Toma esa luz.

COQUÍN   ¿Yo?

DON GUTIERRE   El recelo   1305
pierde, pues conmigo vas.

DOÑA MENCÍA   Villano, ¿cobarde estás?
Saca tú la espada; yo
iré. La luz se cayó.

Al tomar la luz, la mata disimuladamente, y salen Jacinta, y don Enrique siguiéndola.

DON GUTIERRE   Esto me faltaba más;   1310
pero a escuras entraré.

JACINTA *[Ap. a*   Síguete, señor, por mí;
don Enrique]   seguro vas por aquí,
que toda la casa sé.

[Vanse Jacinta y Enrique.]

COQUÍN   ¿Dónde iré yo?

DON GUTIERRE   Ya topé   1315
el hombre.

Coge a Coquín.

DON GUTIERRE   Good God, what is it? What's happened?

DA. MENCÍA   A man –

DON GUTIERRE   Quickly!

DA. MENCÍA   – I've found a man hidden in my room, all cloaked in the darkness. Help, Gutierre!

DON GUTIERRE   What are you saying? My God! Now I'm really worried. A strange man in my house?

DA. MENCÍA   I saw him.

DON GUTIERRE   I'm stunned. Take this light.

COQUÍN   Me?

DON GUTIERRE   Don't be afraid, you're coming with me.

DA. MENCÍA   Fool, are you a coward? Give me your sword; I'll go.
      The light fell!

Taking the light, she secretly extinguishes it. Jacinta enters, with Prince Enrique following her.

DON GUTIERRE   That's just what I needed! But I'll enter anyway, in the dark.

JACINTA   [*Aside to the Prince*] Sir, follow me. I know the whole house, and this way is safe.

[Jacinta and the Prince leave.]

COQUÍN   Where shall I go?

DON GUTIERRE   I've found him.

He seizes Coquín.

1309+   Taking the Light, she secretly extinguishes it: Literally, 'she kills it'. 'Killing the light' / *matar la luz* is a motif in the rest of the play. The translation renders it 'extinguishing' or 'smothering', which flows more smoothly in English. Another possible translation would be 'snuffing out the light'. On *matar la luz*, see Wardropper (1958, pp. 10–11). On lightness/ darkness imagery in the play, see Sloman, p. 52.

1311   I'll enter anyway, in the dark: Cruickshank (1989, 138) suggests that although there are no directions to so indicate, Don Gutierre either heads toward the door, or – as VT has it – very briefly leaves the stage at this point, giving Jacinta the opportunity to speak to Enrique as she leads him out of the house. Gutierre then would re-enter by line 1315. We have chosen to keep Gutierre on the scene, and to have Jacinta speak in an aside to Enrique.

1314+   [*Vanse Jacinta y Enrique.*] / [*Jacinta and Enrique leave.*]: We are adding this stage direction because below (1323+) Jacinta re-enters, with no indication in the Spanish text that she ever left, although her instruction to Enrique (1312-4) makes it obvious that she has taken him off stage.

COQUÍN   Señor, advierte…
DON GUTIERRE ¡Vive Dios, que desta suerte,
              hasta que sepa quién es,
              le he de tener!; que después
              le darán mis manos muerte.   1320
COQUÍN   Mira, que yo…
DOÑA MENCÍA [*Ap.*]   ¡Qué rigor!
              Si es que con él ha topado,
              ¡ay de mí!
DON GUTIERRE   Luz han sacado.

Sale Jacinta con luz.

                          ¿Quién eres, hombre?
COQUÍN   Señor,
              yo soy.
DON GUTIERRE   ¡Qué engaño! ¡Qué error!   1325
COQUÍN   Pues yo ¿no te lo decía?
DON GUTIERRE Que me hablabas presumía;
              pero no que eras el mismo
              que tenía. ¡O ciego abismo
              del alma y paciencia mía!   1330
DOÑA MENCÍA [*Ap. a ella*] ¿Salió ya, Jacinta?
JACINTA   [*Ap. a doña Mencía*]   Sí.
DOÑA MENCÍA Como esto en tu ausencia pasa,
              mira bien toda la casa;
              que como saben que aquí
              no estás, se atreven ansí   1335
              ladrones.
DON GUTIERRE   A verla voy.
              Suspiros al cielo doy,
              que mis sentimientos lleven,
              si es que a mi casa se atreven,
              por ver que en ella no estoy.   1340

[Vánse don Gutierre y Coquín.]

JACINTA   Grande atrevimiento fue
              determinarte, señora,
              a tan grande acción agora.

COQUÍN	Sir, wait –
DON GUTIERRE	By God, I swear I'll hold him like this until I know who he is! And then I'll kill him with my own hands!
COQUÍN	Look –
DA. MENCÍA	[*Aside*] Oh, no! If he's found Enrique, I'm lost!
DON GUTIERRE	Here comes the light.

Jacinta enters with a light.

	Who are you, man?
COQUÍN	Sir, I'm me.
DON GUTIERRE	How frustrating! What a blunder!
COQUÍN	Well, didn't I tell you?
DON GUTIERRE	I knew you were talking to me, but not that you were the one I'd caught. Oh, how infuriating! My patience is stretched to the limit!
DA. MENCÍA	[*Aside to her*] Is he gone yet, Jacinta?
JACINTA	[*Aside to Doña Mencía*] Yes.
DA. MENCÍA	Since this happened while you were gone, please look carefully all through the house. Knowing you're not here, thieves come prowling.
DON GUTIERRE	I'll go look. Heavens above – knowing I'm away they dare to enter my very home.

[Don Gutierre and Coquin go.]

| JACINTA | My lady, it was awfully brave to take such a big risk just now. |

1331+ [*Ap. a doña Mencía*] / [Aside to Doña Mencía]: We add this stage direction, not present in earlier editions, because it suits the secret exchange between Doña Mencía and Jacinta.

1335–6 thieves come prowling: On thieving imagery and the rhetoric of silence in the play, see Daniel Rogers.

1340+ [*Vanse don Gutierre y Coquín.*] / [*Don Gutierre and Coquín go.*]: All previous editions read *Vase*: 'He goes'. We have changed the stage direction because there is no indication of Coquín's – or, for that matter, Jacinta's – exit from this scene. For the forthcoming intimate exchange between husband and wife, we find it improbable that Coquín would remain on stage. Jacinta could go off after her last communication with her mistress, at 1354+, or she could remain on stage until the end of the scene, following Mencía off at 1402+.

DOÑA MENCÍA   En ella mi vida hallé.
JACINTA   ¿Por qué lo hiciste?
DOÑA MENCÍA   Porque   1345
    si yo no se lo dijera
    y Gutierre lo sintiera,
    la presunción era clara,
    pues no se desengañara
    de que yo cómplice era;   1350
      y no fue dificultad
    en ocasión tan cruel,
    haciendo del ladrón fiel,
    engañar con la verdad.

Sale don Gutierre, y debajo de la capa hay una daga.

DON GUTIERRE   ¿Qué ilusión, qué vanidad   1355
    desta suerte te burló?
    Toda la casa vi yo;
    pero en ella no topé
    sombra de que verdad fue
    lo que a ti te pareció.   1360
      ([*Ap.*] Mas es engaño, ¡ay de mí!,
    que esta daga que hallé, ¡cielos!,
    con sospechas y recelos
    previene mi muerte en sí:
    mas no es esto para aquí.)   1365
    Mi bien, mi esposa, Mencía;
    ya la noche en sombra fría
    su manto va recogiendo,
    y cobardemente huyendo
    de la hermosa luz del día.   1370
      Mucho siento, claro está,
    el dejarte en esta parte,
    por dejarte, y por dejarte
    con este temor; mas ya
    es hora.
DOÑA MENCÍA   Los brazos da   1375
    a quien te adora.
DON GUTIERRE   El favor
    estimo.

Al abrazalla, ve la daga.

DA. MENCÍA	It saved my life.
JACINTA	Why did you do it?
DA. MENCÍA	Because if I hadn't told Gutierre someone was there, and he had found out for himself, he'd assume that I was deceiving him. Under such dangerous circumstances, I had to deceive him with the truth.

Don Gutierre enters, and beneath his cape is a dagger.

DON GUTIERRE	What fantasy, what nonsense fooled you this way? I looked through the whole house, but it's clear that what you thought you saw doesn't exist. ([*Aside*] But it's a lie, ah me!, because this dagger I found – heavens! – fills me with suspicions and doom; it foretells my death. But I'll consider this later.)
	My dear, my wife, Mencía, now night gathers up its cloak in cold shadow, and hurries away in fear from the beautiful light of day. I'm so sorry to have to go, both because I hate to leave you, and because I hate to leave you with this fear. But it's time now.
DA. MENCÍA	Please hold the one who adores you.
DON GUTIERRE	I treasure you.

As he embraces her, she sees the dagger.

1353   *haciendo del ladrón fiel:* literally, 'to make the thief an honest man'. Cruickshank (1989, p. 140) cites the proverb, *¿Quieres hacer del ladrón fiel?; fiate dél* (Do you want to make the thief an honest man? Trust him).

1354   *engañar con la verdad* / **deceiving with the truth:** In his *New Art of Writing Plays* (*Arte nuevo de hacer comedias*), p. 163, Lope de Vega enthusiastically recommends this dramatic device.

DOÑA MENCÍA   ¡Tente, señor!
                     ¿Tú la daga para mí?
                     En mi vida te ofendí.
                     Detén la mano al rigor,   1380
                        detén…
DON GUTIERRE   ¿De qué estás turbada,
                     mi bien, mi esposa, Mencía?
DOÑA MENCÍA   Al verte ansí presumía
                     que ya en mi sangre bañada,
                     hoy moría desangrada.   1385
DON GUTIERRE   Como a ver la casa entré,
                     así esta daga saqué.
DOÑA MENCÍA   Toda soy una ilusión.
DON GUTIERRE   ¡Jesús, qué imaginación!
DOÑA MENCÍA   En mi vida te he ofendido.   1390
DON GUTIERRE   ¡Qué necia disculpa ha sido!
                     Pero suele una aprehensión
                        tales miedos prevenir.
DOÑA MENCÍA   Mis tristezas, mis enojos,
                     en tu ausencia estos antojos   1395
                     suelen, mi dueño, fingir.
DON GUTIERRE   Si yo pudiere venir,
                     vendré a la noche, y adiós.
DOÑA MENCÍA   Él vaya, mi bien, con vos.
                     ([*Ap.*] ¡O qué asombros! ¡O qué extremos!)   1400
DON GUTIERRE   [*Ap.*] ¡Ay, honor!, mucho tenemos
                     que hablar a solas los dos.

Vanse cada uno por su puerta.

*Salen el Rey y don Diego con rodela y capa de color; y como representa, se muda
de negro.*

REY   Ten, don Diego, esa rodela.
DON DIEGO   Tarde vienes a acostarte.
REY   Toda la noche rondé   1405
                     de aquesta ciudad las calles;
                     que quiero saber ansí

DA. MENCÍA	Stop, my Lord! You, a dagger for me? I never offended you in my life! Stop, don't be so cruel, stop –
DON GUTIERRE	What is it, my dear, my wife, Mencía?
DA. MENCÍA	Seeing you like that, I thought I was bathed in my own blood, I was dying, bleeding to death.
DON GUTIERRE	When I went to search the house, I took out this dagger.
DA. MENCÍA	I must have been seeing things.
DON GUTIERRE	Blessed Christ, what an imagination!
DA. MENCÍA	I've never offended you in my life.
DON GUTIERRE	What a silly thing to say! But a worry sometimes leads to such fears.
DA. MENCÍA	When you're gone, my lord, my sadness and worry sometimes make me imagine things.
DON GUTIERRE	If I can, I'll come back tonight. Farewell.
DA. MENCÍA	May God go with you, my dearest. ([*Aside*] Oh, what dread, what horror!)
DON GUTIERRE	[*Aside*] Oh, honour! The two of us have a much to discuss in private.

They leave through different doors.

[* *]*

The King, wearing a buckler and red cape, enters with Don Diego; and as they speak, he [the King] changes to a black cape.

KING	Don Diego, take this buckler.
DON DIEGO	You're going to bed late.
KING	All night I made the rounds of the city streets, in order to find

---

1381–92 Cruickshank (1989, p. 142) notes that this passage constitutes a *décima* with two extra lines.

1402+   rodela / buckler: a small round shield carried on the arm. **Red capes** were traditionally worn at night; **black capes** during the day.

1405–06 I made the rounds: As Cruickshank points out (1989, p. 143), to various rulers was attributed the custom of *rondar la ciudad* – making the rounds of the city, usually at night, and often in disguise. See, for example, Lope de Vega's *El castigo sin venganza* (*Punishment without Revenge*), where the Duke of Ferrara does so at the beginning of Act I. See also Shakespeare's *Henry V*, Act IV, scene 1, as the King incognito converses with his men before the battle of Agincourt, testing their mettle and mood.

	sucesos y novedades	
	de Sevilla, que es lugar	
	donde cada noche salen	1410
	cuentos nuevos; y deseo	
	desta manera informarme	
	de todo, para saber	
	lo que convenga.	
DON DIEGO	Bien haces,	
	que el Rey debe ser un Argos	1415
	en su reino, vigilante:	
	el emblema de aquel cetro	
	con dos ojos lo declare.	
	Mas ¿qué vio tu Majestad?	
REY	Vi recatados galanes,	1420
	damas desveladas vi,	
	músicas, fiestas y bailes,	
	muchos garitos, de quien	
	eran siempre voces grandes	
	la tablilla que decía:	1425
	'Aquí hay juego, caminante'.	
	Vi valientes infinitos;	
	y no hay cosa que me canse	
	tanto como ver valientes,	
	y que por oficio pase	1430
	ser uno valiente aquí.	
	Mas porque no se me alaben	
	que no doy examen yo	
	a oficio tan importante,	
	a una tropa de valientes	1435
	probé solo en una calle.	
DON DIEGO	Mal hizo tu Majestad.	
REY	Antes bien, pues con su sangre	
	llevaron iluminada…	
DON DIEGO	¿Qué?	
REY	La carta del examen.	1440

1409 **Seville** was commonly known as a city of rogues and thieves, and was so portrayed in such Golden Age works as Cervantes's *Rinconete y [and] Cortadillo*, Francisco de Quevedo's *La vida del buscón* (*The Rogue's Life*) and Tirso de Molina's *El burlador de Sevilla* (*The Trickster of Seville*).

1415 **Argos:** A giant of Greek mythology famed for his vision.

	out what's happening in Seville. Something new is always going on. That's how I learn about everything, and decide what needs to be done.
DON DIEGO	That's good, because a King ought to be vigilant, an Argos in his land: the emblem on that sceptre with two eyes proclaims it. But what did Your Majesty see?
KING	I saw shifty gallants, I saw women without veils, music, parties and dances, many gambling dens, with signs calling out loudly, 'Here's a game, traveller'. I saw countless hoodlums; and nothing's more tiresome to me than hoodlums, and that being one passes as a profession here. But so that I can't be criticized for not giving an examination for such an important office, I alone tested a whole gang of them in one neighborhood.
DON DIEGO	That's bad, Your Majesty.
KING	On the contrary, it's good, because written in their own blood, they left with –
DON DIEGO	What?
KING	Their graduation diplomas.

1417–8 the emblem on that sceptre with two eyes proclaims it: 'As the result of the invention of printing, emblem books became enormously popular. An emblem was a woodcut of a symbolic picture accompanied by a motto, designed to teach a moral lesson or to be a subject of meditation. The **sceptre with two eyes** means that royal power depends on vigilance' (Wardropper 1970, p. 596). Cf. Diego's remarks to Arias on royal vigilance in Act One, 32–5.

1421 *damas desveladas* / **women without veils:** Honourable women wore veils; those who went uncovered were supposedly shameless. However, in the seventeenth century the veil was believed to be abused. McKendrick writes that in Spain 'on 12 April, 1639, a law was proclaimed, forbidding all women from wearing veils (which, like coaches, were thought to encourage, because they helped conceal, disreputable behaviour) ....' (1974, p. 34). See Perry, p. 150. *Damas desveladas* can also mean women who lose sleep or cause others to lose sleep (Covarrubias, p. 421b): another way of calling them 'brazen'.

1440 *carta de examen* / **graduation diplomas:** Literally, 'letter of examination'. '[F]or important posts an examination of bloodlines was necessary to prove that one's ancestors did not include Moors or Jews. The reference to the blood shed by the hoodlums brings to mind the examination of bloodlines' (Cruickshank, 1989, p. 145). For speculation on this passage in conjunction with Coquín's remarks on the '"Look-Out" family' immediately following, see Cruickshank 1982, p. 34.

Sale Coquín.

COQUÍN	[*Ap.*] No quise entrar en la torre
	con mi amo, por quedarme
	a saber lo que se dice
	de su prisión. Pero, ¡tate!
	(que es un pero muy honrado 1445
	del celebrado linaje
	de los tates de Castilla),
	porque el Rey está delante.
REY	Coquín.
COQUÍN	Señor.
REY	¿Cómo va?
COQUÍN	Responderé a lo estudiante. 1450
REY	¿Cómo?
COQUÍN	*De corpore bene*,
	pero *de pecunis male*.
REY	Decid algo, pues sabéis,
	Coquín, que como me agrade,
	tenéis aquí cien escudos. 1455
COQUÍN	Fuera hacer tú aquesta tarde
	el papel de una comedia
	que se llamaba *El rey ángel*.
	Pero con todo eso traigo
	hoy un cuento que contarte, 1460
	que remata en epigrama.
REY	Si es vuestra, será elegante.
	Vaya el cuento.
COQUÍN	Yo vi ayer
	de la cama levantarse
	un capón con bigotera. 1465
	¿No te ríes de pensarle
	curándose sobre sano
	con tan vagamundo parche?
	A esto un epigrama hice:
	(No te pido, Pedro el grande, 1470
	casas ni viñas; que sólo
	risa pido en este guante:
	dad vuestra bendita risa
	a un gracioso vergonzante.)
	'Floro, casa muy desierta 1475
	la tuya debe de ser,

Coquín enters.

COQUÍN [*Aside*] I refused to go back into the tower with my master, so I could stay behind and find out what they're saying about his imprisonment. But look out! (who's a very honourable 'But' from the celebrated 'Look-Out' family of Castile), because here's the King.

KING Coquín.

COQUÍN Sir.

KING How's it going?

COQUÍN I'll give a student's response.

KING Which is?

COQUÍN *De corpore bene*, but *de pecunis male*.

KING Healthy in body, but sickly in purse? Very well; say something, and if it strikes me as funny, I'll give you one hundred gold coins.

COQUÍN Then you'd deserve the title role in a play called *The Angel King*. Anyway, I have a story to tell you now that ends in an epigram.

KING If it's yours, it will be elegant. Let's hear the story.

COQUÍN Yesterday I saw a eunuch get out of bed wearing a moustache guard. Don't you laugh when you picture him with that useless plaster, curing himself when he's not even sick?

Here's my epigram (Peter the Great, I don't ask you for mansions or vineyards; all I ask for in my collection plate is laughter. Give this silly jester your blessed guffaw): 'Floro, your house must really be deserted. That empty plaster explains

---

1444 *Pero*: The Spanish for 'but' was also a common variation on 'Pedro'.

1458 *The Angel King*: Shergold and Varey (1963, p. 236) report that a play called *The Angel King* was performed at court in 1622. Juan de Mojica wrote two *comedias* (published in 1650) in which *The Angel King* figures in the title. See notes by Jones (p. 56) and Cruickshank (1989, pp. 146–7).

1463–5 A **moustache guard** 'was used when moustaches were in fashion, to put them into, when one was at home or in bed, so that they would not be mussed and spoiled' (*Autoridades* I, p. 608b). It will be noted that eunuchs do not grow facial hair.

1467 **curing himself when he's not even sick**: See line 1243 note, and lines 2392–3.

	porque eso nos da a entender	
	la cédula de la puerta:	
	donde no hay carta, ¿hay cubierta?,	
	¿cáscara sin fruta? No,	1480
	no pierdas tiempo; que yo,	
	esperando los provechos,	
	he visto labrar barbechos,	
	mas barbideshechos no'.	
REY	¡Qué frialdad!	
COQUÍN	Pues adiós, dientes.	1485

Sale el Infante.

DON ENRIQUE	Dadme vuestra mano.	
REY	Infante,	
	¿cómo estáis?	
DON ENRIQUE	Tengo salud,	
	contento de que se halle	
	vuestra Majestad con ella;	
	y esto, señor, a una parte:	1490
	don Arias…	
REY	Don Arias es	
	vuestra privanza: sacalde	
	de la prisión, y haced vos,	
	Enrique, esas amistades,	
	y agradézcanos la vida.	1495
DON ENRIQUE	La tuya los cielos guarden;	
	y heredero de ti mismo,	
	apuestes eternidades	
	con el tiempo.	

Vase el Rey.

	Iréis, don Diego,	
	a la torre, y al alcaide	1500
	le diréis que traiga aquí	
	los dos presos.	

[Vase don Diego.]

	([*Ap.*] Cielos, dadme	
	paciencia en tales desdichas,	
	y prudencia en tales males.)	
	Coquín, ¿tú estabas aquí?	1505

the name-plate on your door: if there's no letter, what good's
an envelope? A rind without the fruit? What a waste of time!
I've seen fallow ground worked to produce a crop, but not a
beardless face'.

KING   How lame!

COQUÍN   Well, *adiós*, teeth of mine!

The Prince enters.

PRINCE   Give me your hand.

KING   Prince Enrique, how are you?

PRINCE   I'm well, and glad to see that Your Majesty is, too. May I speak
to you aside? Don Arias –

KING   Don Arias is your favourite. Take him from the prison, Enrique,
and have him make things right with Gutierre. They should
thank you for their lives.

PRINCE   Sir, may the heavens keep you safe; may you live for eternity.

The King leaves.

Don Diego, go to the tower, and tell the warden to bring the two
prisoners here.

[Don Diego leaves.]

([*Aside*] Heaven give me patience and prudence in all these
setbacks.) Coquín, are you here?

COQUÍN   And better I were in Flanders.

1463–84 On the significance of the joke, coming at the center of the play, see Cruz 2001.

1482   *privanza* refers to the institution of the royal favourite, or the closest adviser/confidante of the royal figure. In this case, Don Arias is the favourite (*privado*) of Prince Enrique.

1498–9 **may you live for eternity:** Literally, 'May you wager eternities with time'.

1506   **Flanders:** In Calderón's time, Flanders was a region in the western part of the Spanish Netherlands. The Dutch revolt against Spain 'lasted longer than any other rebellion in modern European history (1566–1648) and involved more continuous warfare (1572–1609 and 1621–48)' (*The Times Atlas of World History*, 185).

COQUÍN	Y más me valiera en Flandes.
DON ENRIQUE	¿Cómo?
COQUÍN	El Rey es un prodigio
	de todos los animales.
DON ENRIQUE	¿Por qué?
COQUÍN	La naturaleza

permite que el toro brame,   1510
ruja el león, muja el buey,
el asno rebuzne, el ave
cante, el caballo relinche,
ladre el perro, el gato maye,
aulle el lobo, el lechón gruña,   1515
y sólo permitió dalle
risa al hombre, y Aristóteles
risible animal le hace,
por difinición perfeta;
y el Rey, contra el orden y arte,   1520
no quiere reírse. Déme
el cielo, para sacarle
risa, todas las tenazas
del buen gusto y del donaire.

Vase, y sale don Gutierre, y don Arias y don Diego.

DON DIEGO	Ya, señor, están aquí	1525
	los presos.	
DON GUTIERRE	Danos tus plantas.	
DON ARIAS	Hoy al cielo nos levantas.	
DON ENRIQUE	El Rey mi señor de mí	
	(porque humilde le pedí	
	vuestras vidas este día)	1530
	estas amistades fía.	
DON GUTIERRE	El honrar es dado a vos.	

Coteja la daga [que se halló] con la espada [del Infante].

	([*Ap.*] ¿Qué es esto que miro? ¡Ay Dios!)	
DON ENRIQUE	Las manos os dad.	
DON ARIAS	La mía	
	es ésta.	
DON GUTIERRE	Y éstos mis brazos,	1535
	cuyo nudo y lazo fuerte	
	no desatará la muerte,	

PRINCE	Why?
COQUÍN	The King is the strangest creature in the world.
PRINCE	What do you mean?
COQUÍN	Nature permits the bull to bellow, the lion to roar, the ox to low, the ass to bray, the bird to sing, the horse to neigh, the dog to bark, the cat to meow, the wolf to howl, the pig to oink. But man is the only animal that's endowed with laughter, and Aristotle in fact defines man very astutely as the creature that laughs. But the King, against all the rules, doesn't want to laugh. To extract a chuckle from him, may heaven give me forceps made out of good humour and wit!

He leaves. Don Gutierre, Don Arias, and Don Diego enter.

DON DIEGO	Sir, here are the prisoners.
DON GUTIERRE	Allow us to kiss your feet.
DON ARIAS	You are most generous.
PRINCE	I asked my lord the King to spare your lives, and he has trusted me to make peace between you.
DON GUTIERRE	You honour us.

He compares the dagger [that he found] with the [Prince's] sword.

	([*Aside*] What's this I see? Oh, God!)
PRINCE	Take each other's hand.
DON ARIAS	Here is mine.
GUTIERRE	And here are my arms. Let this embrace and fellowship prevail until death breaks them to pieces.

1517–9 Aristotle defines him: According to Cruickshank (1989, p. 150), in *De partibus animalium*, 673a, 7–9.

	sin que los haga pedazos.	
DON ARIAS	Confirmen estos abrazos	
	firme amistad desde aquí.	1540
DON ENRIQUE	Esto queda bien así.	
	Entrambos sois caballeros	
	en acudir los primeros	
	a su obligación; y así	
	está bien el ser amigo	1545
	uno y otro; y quien pensare	
	que no queda bien, repare	
	en que ha de reñir conmigo.	
DON GUTIERRE	A cumplir, señor, me obligo	
	las amistades que juro:	1550
	obedeceros procuro,	
	y pienso que me honraréis	
	tanto, que de mí creeréis	
	lo que de mí estáis seguro.	
	Sois fuerte enemigo vos,	1555
	y cuando lealtad no fuera,	
	por temor no me atreviera	
	a romperlas, ¡vive Dios!	
	Vos y yo para otros dos	
	me estuviera a mí muy bien;	1560
	mostrara entonces también	
	que sé cumplir lo que digo;	
	mas con vos por enemigo,	
	¿quién ha de atreverse?, ¿quién?	
	Tanto enojaros temiera	1565
	el alma cuerda y prudente,	
	que a miraros solamente	
	tal vez aun no me atreviera;	
	y si en ocasión me viera	
	de probar vuestros aceros,	1570
	cuando yo sin conoceros	
	a tal extremo llegara,	
	que se muriera estimara	
	la luz del sol por no veros.	
DON ENRIQUE	([*Ap.*] De sus quejas y suspiros	1575
	grandes sospechas prevengo.)	
	Venid conmigo, que tengo	
	muchas cosas que deciros,	
	don Arias.	

DON ARIAS   Let these embraces confirm our unshakable friendship, from now on.

PRINCE   Well done. You're both gentlemen who understand very well how to fulfill your responsibilities, and so it's fitting that you're friends now. Whoever objects will have to deal with me.

DON GUTIERRE   Sir, I vow to live up to this friendship. I intend to obey you, and you'll see that honouring me so much will prove wise. You're a formidable enemy, and if not out of loyalty, out of fear I'd never dare to violate this friendship, by God! You and I facing off against two others would suit me very well: then, too, I'd show you that I always live up to my word.

       But with you for an enemy, who would dare to challenge you? Who? A wise and prudent soul would so fear to provoke you, that perhaps just one look at you would be enough to stop me. If I found myself in a position to test your steel, if I (without recognizing that it was you) ever came to such an extreme, I would hope the light of the sun would die before I found out who it was.

PRINCE   ([*Aside*] The way he speaks is very suspicious.) Come with me, Don Arias, I have a lot to tell you.

DON ARIAS   Iré a serviros.

[Vanse don Enrique, don Diego y don Arias.]

DON GUTIERRE Nada Enrique respondió;   1580
              sin duda se convenció
              de mi razón. ¡Ay de mí!
              ¿Podré ya quejarme? Sí;
              pero, consolarme, no.
              Ya estoy solo, ya bien puedo   1585
              hablar. ¡Ay Dios!, quién supiera
              reducir sólo a un discurso,
              medir con sola una idea
              tantos géneros de agravios,
              tantos linajes de penas   1590
              como cobardes me asaltan,
              como atrevidos me cercan.
              Agora, agora, valor,
              salga repetido en quejas,
              salga en lágrimas envuelto   1595
              el corazón a las puertas
              del alma, que son los ojos;
              y en ocasión como ésta,
              bien podéis, ojos, llorar:
              no lo dejéis de vergüenza.   1600
              Agora, valor, agora
              es tiempo de que se vea
              que sabéis medir iguales
              el valor y la paciencia.
              Pero cese el sentimiento,   1605
              y a fuerza de honor, y a fuerza
              de valor, aun no me dé
              para quejarme licencia;
              porque adula sus penas
              el que pide a la voz justicia dellas.   1610
              Pero vengamos al caso;
              quizá hallaremos respuesta.
              ¡O ruego a Dios que la haya!
              ¡O plegue a Dios que la tenga!
              Anoche llegué a mi casa,   1615
              es verdad; pero las puertas
              me abrieron luego, y mi esposa
              estaba segura y quieta.

DON ARIAS   At your service, sir.

[The Prince, Don Diego, and Don Arias leave.]

DON GUTIERRE He didn't answer me; I must have convinced him. Ah, me! Can I complain yet? Yes: now I'm alone, now I can speak. Oh, God! If only I could reduce to a single speech, measure with just a single idea so many different grievances, so many kinds of pain that brazenly besiege me, that assault me like cowards.

Now, courage, now you may show yourself, multiplied in my complaints. My heart, come forth drenched in tears to my eyes, windows of my soul. At a time like this, well you may weep, my eyes; don't be ashamed.

Now, courage, now is the time to show that you know how to measure yourself with patience.

But let me banish this emotion, and since I'm a man of honour and courage, I'll stop complaining. He who loudly calls for justice for his afflictions, fawns on them.

But let's get down to the main question; perhaps we'll find an answer. Oh, please God, let there be one! Oh, please, God, let me find it!

Last night I went to my house, it's true; but they opened the door to me at once, and my wife was safe and calm. As for

---

1609–10 Cruickshank (1989, p. 153) notes that these two lines, like 1657–8 and 1711–2, form an *estribillo* (refrain) of seven and eleven syllables, punctuating the *romance* verse.

En cuanto a que me avisaron
de que estaba un hombre en ella,   1620
tengo disculpa en que fue
la que me avisó ella mesma.
En cuanto a que se mató
la luz, ¿qué testigo prueba
aquí que no pudo ser   1625
un caso de contingencia?
En cuanto a que hallé esta daga,
hay criados de quien pueda
ser. En cuanto, ¡ay dolor mío!,
que con la espada convenga   1630
del Infante, puede ser
otra espada como ella;
que no es labor tan extraña
que no hay mil que la parezcan.
Y apurando más el caso,   1635
confieso, ¡ay de mí!, que sea
del Infante, y más confieso
que estaba allí, aunque no fuera
posible dejar de verle;
mas siéndolo, ¿no pudiera   1640
no estar culpada Mencía?;
que el oro es llave maestra
que las guardas de criadas
por instantes nos falsea.
¡O, cuánto me estimo haber   1645
hallado esta sutileza!
Y así acortemos discursos,
pues todos juntos se cierran
en que Mencía es quien es,
y soy quien soy; no hay quien pueda   1650
borrar de tanto esplendor
la hermosura y la pureza.
Pero sí puede, mal digo;
que al sol una nube negra,
si no le mancha, le turba,   1655
si no le eclipsa, le hiela.
¿Qué injusta ley condena
que muera el inocente, que padezca?
A peligro estáis, honor,

the fact that they said there was a man in the house, I have the excuse that it was Mencía herself who told me. As for the fact that the light went out, who's to say that it couldn't have been an accident? As for the fact that I found this dagger, it could belong to a servant. As for the fact that it matches – oh, my God – the Prince's sword, perhaps there's another sword like it. The design isn't so unusual that there mustn't be a thousand like it.

And pressing the case further, I concede – ah, me! – that it could be the Prince's and also that he could have been there, although it would have been impossible not to see him. But that being so, couldn't Mencía still be innocent? After all, gold is the master key that unlocks the treachery of servants. Oh, how glad I am to have remembered this point! So let's cut short our colloquies, because all the evidence taken together leads to the conclusion that Mencía is who she is, and I am who I am. No one can erase the beauty and purity of that fact.

But yes, one can, I'm wrong; because if a black cloud doesn't stain the sun, it darkens it; if not eclipsed, the sun is chilled. What kind of an unjust law is this, that condemns the innocent to suffering and death?

Honour, you are in danger, you're not safe for a single

1642–4 *el oro … nos falsea:* literally, 'gold is the master key that never fails to turn the wards of our guardian maidservants'. A play on words, '*nos falsea*' can also mean 'to pick our locks'.
1649–50 Mencía is who she is, and I am who I am: see line 133 note.

no hay hora en vos que no sea   1660
crítica; en vuestro sepulcro
vivís: puesto que os alienta
la mujer, en ella estáis
pisando siempre la güesa.
Yo os he de curar, honor,   1665
y pues al principio muestra
este primero accidente
tan grave peligro, sea
la primera medicina
cerrar al daño las puertas,   1670
atajar al mal los pasos:
y así os receta y ordena
el médico de su honra
primeramente la dieta
del silencio, que es guardar   1675
la boca, tener paciencia;
luego dice que apliquéis
a vuestra mujer finezas,
agrados, gustos, amores,
lisonjas, que son las fuerzas   1680
defensibles, porque el mal
con el despego no crezca;
que sentimientos, disgustos,
celos, agravios, sospechas
con la mujer, y más propia,   1685
aun más que sanan enferman.
Esta noche iré a mi casa
de secreto, entraré en ella,
por ver qué malicia tiene
el mal; y hasta apurar ésta,   1690
disimularé, si puedo,
esta desdicha, esta pena,
este rigor, este agravio,
este dolor, esta ofensa,
este asombro, este delirio,   1695
este cuidado, esta afrenta,
estos celos… ¿Celos dije?
¡Qué mal hice! Vuelva, vuelva
al pecho la voz; mas no,
que si es ponzoña que engendra   1700

moment; you live at the edge of your tomb: since you depend on a woman's behaviour, you're forever treading on your grave. Honour, I've got to cure you, and since this first accident has been so dangerous, let the first medicine be to shut the doors to the damage, to stop the sickness in its tracks. And so, the physician of his honour prescribes for you, first, a diet of silence: hold your tongue and be patient. Next, he says that you should apply to your wife sweet words, pleasantries, pleasures, love, flattery: these are defensive forces, so that the illness won't worsen due to neglect. Because with women, and especially with one's wife, emotional scenes, arguments, jealousy, criticism, and suspicions sicken more than they cure.

Tonight I'll go secretly to my house, to see how advanced the malady is. Until I find out, I'll conceal (if I can) this worry, this pain, this suffering, this offense, this dread, this delirium, this affront, this jealousy –

Did I say jealousy? What a mistake! I take it back! But no, if it's a poison born in my heart, if it hasn't already killed me from

---

1664 *güesa = huesa.*
1675-6 *guardar / la boca:* A play on words, also meaning 'watch your diet'.

mi pecho, si no me dio
la muerte, ¡ay de mí!, al verterla,
al volverla a mí podrá;
que de la víbora cuentan
que la mata su ponzoña   1705
si fuera de sí la encuentra.
¿Celos dije? Celos dije;
pues basta; que cuando llega
un marido a saber que hay
celos, faltará la ciencia;   1710
y es la cura postrera
que el médico de honor hacer intenta.

Vase y sale don Arias y doña Leonor.

DON ARIAS   No penséis, bella Leonor,
que el no haberos visto fue
porque negar intenté   1715
las deudas que a vuestro honor
 tengo; y acreedor a quien
tanta deuda se previene,
el deudor buscando viene,
no a pagar, porque no es bien   1720
 que necio y loco presuma
que pueda jamás llegar
a satisfacer y dar
cantidad que fue tan suma;
 pero en fin, ya que no pago,   1725
que soy el deudor confieso;
no os vuelvo el rostro, y con eso
la obligación satisfago.
DOÑA LEONOR Señor don Arias, yo he sido
la que obligada de vos,   1730
en las cuentas de los dos,
más interés ha tenido.
 Confieso que me quitasteis
un esposo a quien quería;
mas quizá la suerte mía   1735
por ventura mejorasteis;
 pues es mejor que sin vida,
sin opinión, sin honor
viva, que no sin amor,
de un marido aborrecida.   1740

within (my God!), then it will kill me from the outside. It's like the viper: if he ejects his poison and then comes across it afterwards, it will kill him.

Did I say jealousy? I said jealousy. But that's enough: because when a married man comes to realize that he's jealous, his science will fail him, and the physician of honour will attempt the final cure.

He leaves.

[* *]*

Don Arias and Doña Leonor enter.

DON ARIAS	Lovely Leonor, because I failed to come to you sooner, I hope you don't think I was trying to deny the debt I owe your honour. This debtor seeks out the creditor to whom he owes so much: not to repay you for the damage I've caused, because it would be foolish and absurd to think that I could ever restore to you such a great loss. Since I can't pay you back, I remain in your debt, and so I've come to face you and do the best I can to satisfy my obligation.
DA. LEONOR	Don Arias, if we're talking about debts, I'm the one who owes you; I owe more interest on the debt. It's true that you took from me a man I loved, but perhaps it was all for the best. It's better to go on without a life, without a reputation, without honour, than without love, hated by a husband. It was my own fault and

Yo tuve la culpa, yo
la pena siento, y así
sólo me quejo de mí
y de mi estrella.

DON ARIAS   Eso no;
quitarme, Leonor hermosa,   1745
la culpa, es querer negar
a mis deseos lugar;
pues si mi pena amorosa
os significo, ella diga
en cifra sucinta y breve   1750
que es vuestro amor quien me mueve,
mi deseo quien me obliga
a deciros que pues fui
causa de penas tan tristes,
si esposo por mí perdistes,   1755
tengáis esposo por mí.

DOÑA LEONOR   Señor don Arias, estimo,
como es razón, la elección;
y aunque con tanta razón
dentro del alma la imprimo,   1760
licencia me habéis de dar
de responderos también
que no puede estarme bien;
no, señor, porque a ganar
no llegaba yo infinito,   1765
sino porque, si vos fuisteis
quien a Gutierre le disteis
de un mal formado delito
la ocasión, y agora viera
que me casaba con vos,   1770
fácilmente entre los dos
de aquella sospecha hiciera
evidencia; y disculpado,
con demostración tan clara,
con todo el mundo quedara   1775
de haberme a mí despreciado:
y yo estimo de manera
el quejarme con razón,
que no he de darle ocasión
a la disculpa primera;   1780
porque si en un lance tal

I feel the pain. So I only complain about myself and my unlucky star.

DON ARIAS   I disagree. To absolve me of guilt, beautiful lady, is to deny the genuine desire that moves me to speak now. Let me explain: clearly and simply, I'm in love with you. And since I caused your sad situation, since I made you lose a husband, in me you'll gain one.

DA. LEONOR   Don Arias, of course I appreciate the gesture. And although I'm moved to my very soul, I must also say that it wouldn't be good for me. Not because I wouldn't gain infinitely from such a union, but because Gutierre jumped to the wrong conclusion precisely about you. If he saw now that we were marrying, he'd think there had been good reason for his suspicion. And on such clear evidence, the whole world would agree with him; they'd condemn me. I must be able to justify my complaint before the world, and I have no intention of giving him any excuse to claim innocence.

1748–53 *si mi pena amorosa … me obliga / a deciros que …*: Literally, 'let it [my loving concern] say briefly and in short that it's your love that moves me, my desire that compels me to tell you that …'.
1755 *perdistes* = *perdisteis*.

le culpan cuantos le ven,
no han de pensar que hizo bien
quien yo pienso que hizo mal.

DON ARIAS   Frívola respuesta ha sido   1785
la vuestra, bella Leonor;
pues cuando de antiguo amor
os hubiera convencido
  la experiencia, ella también
disculpa en la enmienda os da.   1790
¿Cuánto peor os estará
que tenga por cierto quien
  imaginó vuestro agravio,
y no le constó después
la satisfacción?

DOÑA LEONOR   No es   1795
amante prudente y sabio,
  don Arias, quien aconseja
lo que en mi daño se ve;
pues si agravio entonces fue,
no por eso agora deja   1800
  de ser agravio también,
y peor cuanto haber sido
de imaginado a creído;
y a vos no os estará bien
  tampoco.

DON ARIAS   Como yo sé   1805
la inocencia de ese pecho
en la ocasión, satisfecho
siempre de vos estaré.
  En mi vida he conocido
galán necio, escrupuloso,   1810
y con extremo celoso,
que en llegando a ser marido
  no le castiguen los cielos.
Gutierre pudiera bien
decirlo, Leonor; pues quien   1815
levantó tantos desvelos
  de un hombre en la ajena casa,
extremos pudiera hacer
mayores, pues llega a ver
lo que en la propia le pasa.   1820

Everyone who knows about it holds him responsible now, and I'm not about to let him escape the blame.

DON ARIAS Lovely Leonor, a bad experience in love keeps you from thinking this through, because it should lead you to see the advantage of my offer. How much worse can it be for you if the man who believed the worst about you on flimsy evidence, continues to do so?

DA. LEONOR Don Arias, a lover who advises me to do something that will damage my reputation is neither prudent nor wise. What was an offense then will remain one now, and will be even worse because it will be not just suspected, but positively believed. It won't be good for you, either.

DON ARIAS Since I know you were innocent, I'll always trust you. I've never in my life met a foolish, demanding, extremely jealous lover who wasn't punished by the heavens when he married. Gutierre could certainly tell you that, Leonor. The fellow who was so obsessed about a man in someone else's house, would go wild if he found out what was happening in his own house.

DOÑA LEONOR Señor don Arias, no quiero
escuchar lo que decís;
que os engañáis, o mentís.
Don Gutierre es caballero
 que en todas las ocasiones,   1825
con obrar, y con decir,
sabrá, vive Dios, cumplir
muy bien sus obligaciones;
 y es hombre cuya cuchilla,
o cuyo consejo sabio,   1830
sabrá no sufrir su agravio
ni a un Infante de Castilla.
 Si pensáis vos que con eso
mis enojos aduláis,
muy mal, don Arias, pensáis;   1835
y si la verdad confieso,
 mucho perdisteis conmigo;
pues si fuerais noble vos,
no hablárades, vive Dios,
así de vuestro enemigo.   1840
 Y yo, aunque ofendida estoy,
y aunque la muerte le diera
con mis manos, si pudiera,
no le murmurara hoy
 en el honor, desleal;   1845
sabed, don Arias, que quien
una vez le quiso bien,
no se vengará en su mal.

Vase.

DON ARIAS   No supe qué responder.
Muy grande ha sido mi error,   1850
pues en escuelas de honor
arguyendo una mujer
 me convence. Iré al Infante,
y humilde le rogaré
que destos cuidados dé   1855
parte ya de aquí adelante
 a otro; y porque no lo yerre,
ya que el día va a morir,
me ha de matar, o no he de ir
en casa de don Gutierre.   1860

DA. LEONOR	Don Arias, I refuse to listen to this. Either you're mistaken, sir, or you lie. By heaven, Don Gutierre is a gentleman who always knows, in deeds and in words, how to fulfill his responsibilities; and he's a man whose weapon, or whose wisdom, won't shrink from answering an insult, even from a Prince of Castile.
	Don Arias, if you think that you curry my favour with such allegations, you think wrong. And to tell the truth, I'm very disappointed in you, because if you were noble, by heaven!, you wouldn't speak that way about your enemy.
	And although he offended me, and I'd kill him with my own hands if I could, I wouldn't slander him, I wouldn't cast slurs on his honour. Know, Don Arias, that she who once loved him truly, will not take revenge in his affliction.
She leaves.	
DON ARIAS	I didn't know what to say. I've certainly had it wrong, if in the school of honour a woman can teach me about my error. I'll go to the Prince, and beg him humbly but firmly, from now on to find someone else to help with these matters of the heart. Daylight is fading. I must make him see that even if he kills me, I won't go to Don Gutierre's house.

1850–3 I've certainly had it wrong ... about my error: It will be recalled that in Act One, Don Arias, angry that he had allowed himself to be hidden in a room of Leonor's house upon the courting Gutierre's arrival, laid a curse on the man who follows a woman's advice (968–70).

1857 *porque no lo yerre*: Jones (p. 70) believes that it means *para que no deje de hacerlo*: 'so that he will not fail to do it'.

Vase.

Sale don Gutierre, como [quien salta] unas tapias.

DON GUTIERRE	En el mudo silencio
	de la noche, que adoro y reverencio
	por sombra aborrecida,
	como sepulcro de la humana vida,
	de secreto he venido	1865
	hasta mi casa, sin haber querido
	avisar a Mencía
	de que ya libertad del Rey tenía,
	para que descuidada
	estuviese, ¡ay de mí!, desta jornada.	1870
	Médico de mi honra
	me llamo, pues procuro mi deshonra
	curar; y así he venido
	a visitar mi enfermo, a hora que ha sido
	de ayer la misma, ¡cielos!,	1875
	a ver si el accidente de mis celos
	a su tiempo repite.
	El dolor mis intentos facilite.
	Las tapias de la huerta
	salté, porque no quise por la puerta	1880
	entrar. ¡Ay Dios, qué introducido engaño
	es en el mundo no querer su daño
	examinar un hombre,
	sin que el recelo ni el temor le asombre!
	Dice mal quien lo dice;	1885
	que no es posible, no, que un infelice
	no llore sus desvelos:
	mintió quien dijo que calló con celos,
	o confiéseme aquí que no los siente.
	Mas ¡sentir y callar!: otra vez miente.	1890
	Este es el sitio donde
	suele de noche estar; aun no responde
	el eco entre estos ramos.
	Vamos pasito, honor, que ya llegamos;
	que en estas ocasiones	1895
	tienen los celos pasos de ladrones.

Descubre una cortina donde está durmiendo [doña Mencía].

He leaves.

[* *]*

Don Gutierre enters, as if vaulting a wall.

DON GUTIERRE   I worship the night, abhorrent shadow, sepulchre of all human life. In the mute silence, I've come secretly to my house. I didn't send Mencía word that the King has let me go, so that she wouldn't be prepared for my journey here. I call myself the physician of my honour, because I intend to cure my dishonour, and so I've come to visit my sick patient at the same hour as yesterday (oh, God!) to see if jealousy will suddenly attack again. My suffering makes this mission easier. I've leapt over the garden walls instead of going in through the door.

Oh, God, how fear and suspicion plague the man investigating his injury! He can't help but weep over his grievances. Whoever claimed he could keep quiet about an attack of jealousy lied – either that, or he'd have to admit that he wasn't really jealous. To feel it and remain silent – impossible!

This is where she usually spends the evening; not a sound rustles among these branches. Let's go softly, honour, now we're here; at times like this, jealousy takes the footsteps of a thief.

He opens a curtain where [Doña Mencía] is asleep.

1870   *jornada*: Could mean 'journey', 'occasion', or the theatrical noun 'act' – the *comedia* typically is divided into three *jornadas*, or *actos*. Don Gutierre's remark may thus be seen to draw attention to the theatricality of this play. For other instances and some implications of self-referentiality as a 'generic component' of *The Physician of His Honour*, see Simerka.
1896   jealousy takes the footsteps of a thief: See lines 1335–6 note.
1896+ *He opens a curtain where [Doña Mencía] is asleep*: Here Don Gutierre probably opens the center curtain, as he will twice more (lines 2457+ and 2871+). On staging the discoveries, see 'Staging and Setting' in Introduction.

¡Ay, hermosa Mencía,
qué mal tratas mi amor, y la fe mía!
Volverme otra vez quiero.
Bueno he hallado mi honor, hacer no quiero   1900
por agora otra cura,
pues la salud en él está segura.
Pero ¿ni una criada
la acompaña? ¿Si acaso retirada
aguarda…? ¡O pensamiento   1905
injusto! ¡O vil temor! ¡O infame aliento!
Ya con esta sospecha
no he de volverme; y pues que no aprovecha
tan grave desengaño,
apuremos de todo en todo el daño.   1910
Mato la luz, y llego
sin luz y sin razón, dos veces ciego;
pues bien encubrir puedo
el metal de la voz, hablando quedo.
¡Mencía!

Despiértala.

DOÑA MENCÍA   ¡Ay Dios! ¿Qué es esto?
DON GUTIERRE   No des voces.   1915
DOÑA MENCÍA   ¿Quién es?
DON GUTIERRE   Yo soy, mi bien. ¿No me conoces?
DOÑA MENCÍA   Sí, señor; que no fuera
                    otro tan atrevido…
DON GUTIERRE   [*Ap.*] Ella me ha conocido.
DOÑA MENCÍA   …que así hasta aquí viniera.   1920
                    ¿Quién hasta aquí llegara
                    que no fuérades vos, que no dejara
                    en mis manos la vida,
                    con valor y con honra defendida?
DON GUTIERRE   ([*Ap.*] ¡Qué dulce desengaño!   1925
                    ¡Bien haya, amén, el que apuró su daño!)
                    Mencía, no te espantes de haber visto
                    tal extremo.
DOÑA MENCÍA   ¡Qué mal, temor, resisto
                    el sentimiento!
DON GUTIERRE   Mucha razón tiene
                    tu valor.

Oh, lovely Mencía, how you try my love and my trust!

I'll turn back now: I've found my honour safe and in good health, and I don't need to cure it for now.

But not a single maidservant is with her? Can she be waiting here alone ...? Oh, unjust thought! Oh, vile fear! Oh, loathsome idea! Now that I have this suspicion, I can't turn back, and since such compelling evidence of her innocence is still insufficient, let's fully examine the injury. I'll put out the lamp, and I'll come in without light or logic, twice blinded. Speaking quietly, I'll disguise my voice.

Mencía!

He awakens her.

DA. MENCÍA	Oh, God! What's this?
DON GUTIERRE	Don't cry out.
DA. MENCÍA	Who is it?
DON GUTIERRE	It's me, darling. Don't you know me?
DA. MENCÍA	Yes, sir, no one else –
DON GUTIERRE	[*Aside*] She's recognized me.
DA. MENCÍA	– would dare come in here. Anyone else I would have fought to the death, bravely and with honour.
DON GUTIERRE	([*Aside*] What a sweet revelation! Happy the man who investigates an injury, amen!) Mencía, don't worry about my unusual behaviour.
DA. MENCÍA	I'm so afraid!
DON GUTIERRE	You've proven your courage.

1926   *amén* / amen: We follow Cruickshank's suggestion (1989, p. 165) that *amén* rather than *amor* (love) is the more appropriate reading here. He bases the conjecture on the *amén* in VT, which contradicts amor in QC, S, and Q, and on the correspondence of this line with 968-69 in Act One: **Mil veces mal haya, amén, / quien de una mujer se rinde / a admitir el parecer!** (**A thousand curses on the man who follows a woman's advice, amen!**).

DOÑA MENCÍA	¿Qué disculpa me previene…	1930
DON GUTIERRE	Ninguna.	
DOÑA MENCÍA	…de venir así tu Alteza?	
DON GUTIERRE	[*Ap.*]¡Tu Alteza! No es conmigo, ¡ay Dios! ¿Qué escucho?	

Con nuevas dudas lucho.
¡Qué pesar! ¡Qué desdicha! ¡Qué tristeza!

DOÑA MENCÍA ¿Segunda vez pretende ver mi muerte? 1935
¿Piensa que cada día…
DON GUTIERRE [*Ap.*] ¡O trance fuerte!
DOÑA MENCÍA …puede esconderse…
DON GUTIERRE [*Ap.*] ¡Cielos!
DOÑA MENCÍA …y matando la luz…
DON GUTIERRE [*Ap.*] ¡Matadme, celos!
DOÑA MENCÍA …salir a riesgo mío
delante de Gutierre?
DON GUTIERRE [*Ap.*] Desconfío 1940
de mí, pues que dilato
morir, y con mi aliento no la mato.
El venir no ha extrañado
el Infante, ni dél se ha recatado,
sino sólo ha sentido 1945
que en ocasión se ponga, ¡estoy perdido!,
de que otra vez se esconda.
¡Mi venganza a mi agravio corresponda!
DOÑA MENCÍA Señor, vuélvase luego.
DON GUTIERRE [*Ap.*] ¡Ay, Dios! Todo soy rabia, y todo fuego. 1950
DOÑA MENCÍA Tu Alteza así otra vez no llegue a verse.
DON GUTIERRE ¿Que por eso no más ha de volverse?
DOÑA MENCÍA Mirad que es hora que Gutierre venga.
DON GUTIERRE ([*Ap.*] ¿Habrá en el mundo quien paciencia tenga?
Sí, si prudente alcanza 1955
oportuna ocasión a su venganza.)
No vendrá; yo le dejo entretenido;
y guárdame un amigo
las espaldas el tiempo que conmigo
estáis: él no vendrá, yo estoy seguro. 1960

Sale Jacinta.

JACINTA [Ap.] Temerosa procuro
ver quién hablaba aquí.
DOÑA MENCÍA Gente he sentido.

DA. MENCÍA	What excuse do you have –
DON GUTIERRE	None.
DA. MENCÍA	– for coming like this, Your Highness?
DON GUTIERRE	[*Aside*] 'Your Highness!' Oh, God, what's she saying? She's not speaking to me! Now what do I do? What a blow! What bad news! Oh, what agony!
DA. MENCÍA	Again you risk my life? Do you think that every day –
DON GUTIERRE	[*Aside*] Oh, no!
DA. MENCÍA	– you can hide –
DON GUTIERRE	[*Aside*] My God!
DA. MENCÍA	– and smothering the light –
DON GUTIERRE	[*Aside*] This jealousy is smothering me!
DA. MENCÍA	– you can walk out right past Gutierre, putting me in such danger?
DON GUTIERRE	[*Aside*] Why don't I just die now, and kill her with my last breath? She's not surprised that the Prince has come, and she hasn't pulled away from him. She's only sorry that she has to hide him again. That does it! Let my revenge match the offense!
DA. MENCÍA	Sir, go away right now.
DON GUTIERRE	[*Aside*] Oh, God! I'm burning with rage!
DA. MENCÍA	Your Highness, don't ever come here like this again.
DON GUTIERRE	Is that the only reason not to come back?
DA. MENCÍA	Look, Gutierre may come now.
DON GUTIERRE	([*Aside*] Would anyone in the world stand for this? Yes – if he waited for the right time to take revenge.) He won't come; when I left him he was busy, and a friend of mine is watching outside while I'm with you. He won't come, I'm sure of it.

Jacinta enters.

JACINTA	[*Aside*] Something's wrong: I'm trying to find out who was talking here.
DA. MENCÍA	I've heard someone.

DON GUTIERRE ¿Qué haré?
DOÑA MENCÍA   ¿Qué? Retirarte,
              no a mi aposento, sino a otra parte.

Vase don Gutierre detrás del paño.

              ¡Hola!
JACINTA   ¿Señora?
DOÑA MENCÍA   El aire que corría   1965
              entre estos ramos mientras yo dormía,
              la luz ha muerto; luego
              traed luces.

Vase Jacinta.

DON GUTIERRE ([*Ap.*]   Encendidas en mi fuego.
              Si aquí estoy escondido,
              han de verme, y de todas conocido,   1970
              podrá saber Mencía
              que he llegado a entender la pena mía;
              y porque no lo entienda,
              y dos veces me ofenda,
              una con tal intento,   1975
              y otra pensando que lo sé y consiento,
              dilatando su muerte,
              he de hacer la deshecha desta suerte.)

Dice dentro.

              ¡Hola! ¿Cómo está aquí desta manera?
DOÑA MENCÍA   Éste es Gutierre: otra desdicha espera   1980
              mi espíritu cobarde.
DON GUTIERRE ¿No han encendido luces, y es tan tarde?

Sale Jacinta con luz, y don Gutierre por otra puerta de donde se escondió.

JACINTA   Ya la luz está aquí.
DON GUTIERRE   ¡Bella Mencía!
DOÑA MENCÍA   ¡O mi esposo! ¡O mi bien! ¡O gloria mía!
DON GUTIERRE [*Ap.*] ¡Qué fingidos extremos!   1985
              Mas, alma y corazón, disimulemos.
DOÑA MENCÍA   Señor, ¿por dónde entrasteis?
DON GUTIERRE   Desa huerta,
              con la llave que tengo, abrí la puerta.

DON GUTIERRE What should I do?

DA. MENCÍA What? Get back, not to my room – somewhere else.

Gutierre goes behind the curtain.

Hello!

JACINTA Madam?

DA. MENCÍA The breeze that runs along these branches put out the light while I was sleeping; bring more lights right away.

Jacinta leaves.

DON GUTIERRE ([*Aside*] Lights burning with my fire. If I'm hidden here, they'll see me, and then Mencía will know that I know what's going on. If she finds out that I know, I'll be twice offended – once because she's deceived me; and again, that she thinks I consent to her affair because I know about it and don't kill her right away. I've got to keep secret what I plan to do.)

He says within.

Hello! What's going on here?

DA. MENCÍA This is Gutierre: now I'm even more frightened of what will happen.

DON GUTIERRE No lights yet, and it's so late?

Jacinta enters with a light, and Don Gutierre comes in through another door, behind which he'd been hiding.

JACINTA Here's the light.

DON GUTIERRE Lovely Mencía!

DA. MENCÍA Oh, my husband! Oh, my dearest! Oh, my beloved!

DON GUTIERRE [*Aside*] What a false display! But, my soul and my heart, let us pretend, too.

DA. MENCÍA Sir, where did you come in?

DON GUTIERRE From the outer garden, I opened the gate with the key. My wife,

---

1964+ *Gutierre goes behind the curtain:* Although Calderón uses *paño* for curtain instead of the earlier *cortina*, we can assume that Gutierre steps partly or completely behind one of the interior curtains. See Introduction: 'Staging and Setting'.

1978+ He says within: In other words, 'From behind the curtain, he says'.

Mi esposa, mi señora,
¿en qué te entretenías?

DOÑA MENCÍA   Vine agora   1990
a este jardín, y entre estas fuentes puras,
dejóme el aire a escuras.

DON GUTIERRE No me espanto, bien mío;
que el aire que mató la luz, tan frío
corre, que es un aliento   1995
respirado del céfiro violento,
y que no sólo advierte
muerte a las luces, a las vidas muerte,
y pudieras dormida
a sus soplos también perder la vida.   2000

DOÑA MENCÍA Entenderte pretendo,
y aunque más lo procuro, no te entiendo.

DON GUTIERRE ¿No has visto ardiente llama
perder la luz al aire que la hiere,
y que a este tiempo de otra luz inflama   2005
la pavesa? Una vive y otra muere
a sólo un soplo. Así, desta manera
la lengua de los vientos lisonjera
matarte la luz pudo,
y darme luz a mí.

DOÑA MENCÍA ([*Ap.*]   El sentido dudo.)   2010
Parece que celoso
hablas en dos sentidos.

DON GUTIERRE ([*Ap.*]   Riguroso
es el dolor de agravios;
mas con celos ningunos fueron sabios.)
¿Celoso? ¿Sabes tú lo que son celos?   2015
Que yo no sé qué son, ¡viven los cielos!;
porque si lo supiera,
y celos…

DOÑA MENCÍA [*Ap.*]   ¡Ay de mí!

DON GUTIERRE   …llegar pudiera
a tener… ¿qué son celos?
átomos, ilusiones, y desvelos;…   2020
no más que de una esclava, una criada,
por sombra imaginada,
con hechos inhumanos,
a pedazos sacara con mis manos

	my lady, how were you passing the time?
DA. MENCÍA	I just came to the garden, and the breeze blew out the flame, leaving me in the dark among these fountains.
DON GUTIERRE	That doesn't surprise me, my dear, because the air that extinguished the light runs so cold that it's the breath of a violent zephyr. It foretells not only the death of lights, but of lives. While sleeping, you could also lose your life to the breeze.
DA. MENCÍA	I don't understand.
DON GUTIERRE	Haven't you seen a fierce flame lose its light to the air that cuts through it, while at the same time kindling the embers of another blaze? With a single puff, one lives and the other dies. This is how the wind's flattering tongue could extinguish your light, and give light to me.
DA. MENCÍA	(*[Aside]* I don't understand him.) You speak with hidden meanings; you seem to be jealous.
DON GUTIERRE	(*[Aside]* This pain is outrageous. But with jealousy, no men are wise.)
	Jealous? Do you know what jealousy is? I don't know what it is, by heaven! Because if I did know, and jealousy –
DA. MENCÍA	*[Aside]* Ah, me!
DON GUTIERRE	– did come to possess me – what is jealousy? Atoms, illusions, anxieties – of no more than a slave woman, or a maidservant, because of an imagined shadow – with inhuman force, I would rip out her heart in pieces with my own hands; and then, drenched

1996   zephyr: A gentle breeze from the west.
2003–10 Haven't you seen … give light to me: On this image in emblematics, see Cull, pp. 117–8.

	el corazón, y luego	2025
	envuelto en sangre, desatado en fuego,	
	el corazón comiera	
	a bocados, la sangre me bebiera,	
	el alma le sacara,	
	y el alma,¡vive Dios!, despedazara,	2030
	si capaz de dolor el alma fuera.	
	¿Pero cómo hablo yo desta manera?	
DOÑA MENCÍA	Temor al alma ofreces.	
DON GUTIERRE	¡Jesús, Jesús mil veces!	
	¡Mi bien, mi esposa, cielo, gloria mía!	2035
	¡Ah mi dueño! ¡Ah Mencía!	
	Perdona, por tus ojos,	
	esta descompostura, estos enojos;	
	que tanto un fingimiento	
	fuera de mí llevó mi pensamiento;	2040
	y vete, por tu vida; que prometo	
	que te miro con miedo y con respeto,	
	corrido deste exceso.	
	¡Jesús! No estuve en mí, no tuve seso.	
DOÑA MENCÍA	[*Ap.*] Miedo, espanto, temor, y horror tan fuerte,	2045
	parasismos han sido de mi muerte.	
DON GUTIERRE	[*Ap.*] Pues médico me llamo de mi honra,	
	yo cubriré con tierra mi deshonra.	

[Vanse.]

2024–32 I would eat her heart … tear it to pieces: 'Although his fury may prevent him from realizing it, these words of Don Gutierre recall holy communion; thus we see that the cult of honour practiced by Don Gutierre is at the same time a parody and a negation of the Christian religion' (Cruickshank 1989, p. 171). See also Cruickshank's 'Metaphorical *Criptojudaísmo*', pp. 36–7.

2034   *¡Jesús, Jesús mil veces!* / Jesus, Lord Jesus!: Gutierre repeats almost exactly the opening line of the play, Prince Enrique's exclamation as he falls.

2036   *Dueño*: Literally, 'owner'. See line 214 note.

in blood, unbound in fire, I would eat her heart by mouthfuls, I would drink her blood, I would rip out her soul, and if her soul were capable of pain, I swear to God! I would tear it to pieces. But how can I be speaking like this?

DA. MENCÍA   You bring fear to my soul.

DON GUTIERRE   Jesus, Lord Jesus! My dearest, my wife, my heaven, my glory! Ah, my mistress! Ah, Mencía! Upon your soul, pardon this outburst: my imagination carried me away. Upon your life, do go in. I swear to you, I regard you with fear and respect. I'm ashamed of this display. Lord Jesus! I was beside myself, I was out of my mind.

DA. MENCÍA   [*Aside*] Fear, shock, dread, and such immense horror: I feel converging on me the convulsions of my own death.

DON GUTIERRE   [*Aside*] Since I call myself the physician of my honour, I'll bury my dishonour in the ground.

[*They leave.*]

2041   [*V*]*ete, por tu vida* / **Upon your life, do go in:** Literally, 'Go, for your life's sake'. The phrase can be taken simply as a forceful exhortation, or alternatively as an exhortation masking a threat.

2045–8 Fear, shock, dread ... in the ground [*tierra*]: Dámaso Alonso points out (p. 153) that in Calderón's *comedias*, often at the conclusion of a scene, and particularly at the end of the second act, key characters make declarations that are structurally parallel, although the meanings diverge according to the situation of the speaker. Such a device is highly dramatic; it also serves, Alonso writes, 'to condense in the imagination of the spectator the workings of the plot'.

Additionally, it will be noted that Gutierre's final utterance recalls the cosmic element that occupies the opening lines of Act II, where Prince Enrique assures Jacinta that his feet 'barely touch the ground [*tierra*]' (1021–2).

And finally, Cruickshank (1982, p. 35) links Gutierre's covering his dishonour with earth here and on lines 2097–8 to the Jewish 'ritual killing of animals to be eaten: Jews would cut their throats, allow the blood to drain away, ant then cover it with earth'. On the possible significance of this practice for the play, see Cruickshank 1982, p. 35. Melveena McKendrick (1994) and more recently, Georgina Dopico Black (2001) have argued that the obsession with honour in the wife-murder *comedias* is really a 'mimetic transference' of seventeenth-century Spanish preoccupation with *limpieza de sangre*.

TERCERA JORNADA

Sale todo el acompañamiento, y don Gutierre y el Rey.

DON GUTIERRE   Pedro, a quien el indio polo
                coronar de luz espera,   2050
                hablarte a solas quisiera.
REY   Idos todos.

Vase el acompañamiento.

                     Ya estoy solo.
DON GUTIERRE Pues a ti, español Apolo,
                a ti, castellano Atlante,
                en cuyos hombros, constante,   2055
                se ve durar y vivir
                todo un orbe de zafir,
                todo un globo de diamante:
                  a ti, pues, rindo en despojos
                la vida mal defendida   2060
                de tantas penas, si es vida
                vida con tantos enojos.
                No te espantes que los ojos
                también se quejen, señor;
                que dicen que amor y honor   2065
                pueden, sin que a nadie asombre,
                permitir que llore un hombre;
                y yo tengo honor y amor:
                  honor, que siempre he guardado
                como noble y bien nacido,   2070
                y amor que siempre he tenido
                como esposo enamorado:
                adquirido y heredado
                uno y otro en mí se ve,
                hasta que tirana fue   2075
                la nube, que turbar osa
                tanto esplandor en mi esposa,
                y tanto lustre en su fe.
                  No sé cómo signifique
                mi pena; turbado estoy…   2080
                y más cuando a decir voy

ACT THREE

Don Gutierre, the King, and attendants enter.

DON GUTIERRE King Pedro, destined to shine like a beacon of light throughout the world, from one pole to the other, I would like to speak with you alone.

KING Everyone leave.

Attendants leave.

Now I'm alone.

DON GUTIERRE Then to you, Spanish Apollo, to you, Castilian Atlas, whose shoulders carry an entire orb, a planet of sapphire, a globe of diamond, constant and enduring:

to you, then, I submit my life (if this can be called living), in ruins. I don't know how to fend off so many troubles. Don't be shocked that my eyes describe my pain, sir; they say no one is surprised if love and honour bring a man to tears. I have both honour and love:

honour, which I've always protected as a noble and well-born man; and love – I'm a man in love. I inherited one, and became the other; both were there for everyone to see, until a despotic cloud loomed to defile the lustre of my wife's constancy.

I don't know how to express my pain; I'm in turmoil… and even more now that I'm about to ask you to impose the rigor of

---

2049–108 Act Three begins with *décimas*, ten-line stanzas of eight syllables per line, with consonant rhyme following a consistent pattern and often with a natural pause after the fourth line. Don Gutierre's long speech lends itself to paragraphic divisions by *décimas*. Lope de Vega writes that this kind of verse is 'good for complainings' (*las décimas son buenas para quejas*); see 'Versification' in Introduction, and line 1354 note.

2049–50 *a quien el indio polo / coronar de luz espera* / who is destined to shine like a beacon of light:Literally, 'whom the Indian pole waits to crown with light'. Wardropper (1970, p. 602) writes that '*polo* could be used to mean any region of the earth covered by a pole of a heavenly body, especially the polestar', and suggests that 'light' means 'glory', which in turn means 'empire'. Don Gutierre's statement is prescient in the fourteenth century, but would be appreciated by a seventeenth-century Spanish audience.

2053–4 Apollo: Greek god of light, youth, beauty, and prophecy, among other things; later confused with Helios, the sun god. **Atlas:** see line 675 note.

　　　　　que fue vuestro hermano Enrique
　　　　　contra quien pido se aplique
　　　　　desa justicia el rigor:
　　　　　no porque sepa, señor,　　　　　　　　　　　2085
　　　　　que el poder mi honor contrasta;
　　　　　pero imaginarlo basta,
　　　　　quien sabe que tiene honor.
　　　　　　La vida de vos espero
　　　　　de mi honra; así la curo　　　　　　　　　　2090
　　　　　con prevención, y procuro
　　　　　que ésta la sane primero;
　　　　　porque si en rigor tan fiero
　　　　　malicia en el mal hubiera,
　　　　　junta de agravios hiciera,　　　　　　　　　2095
　　　　　a mi honor desahuciara,
　　　　　con la sangre le lavara,
　　　　　con la tierra le cubriera.
　　　　　　No os turbéis; con sangre digo
　　　　　solamente de mi pecho.　　　　　　　　　　2100
　　　　　Enrique, está satisfecho
　　　　　que está seguro conmigo;
　　　　　y para esto hable un testigo:
　　　　　esta daga, esta brillante
　　　　　lengua de acero elegante,　　　　　　　　　2105
　　　　　suya fue; ved este día
　　　　　si está seguro, pues fía
　　　　　de mí su daga el Infante.
REY　　　　　Don Gutierre, bien está;
　　　　　y quien de tan invencible　　　　　　　　　2110
　　　　　honor corona las sienes,
　　　　　que con los rayos compiten
　　　　　del sol, satisfecho viva
　　　　　de que su honor…
DON GUTIERRE　　　　　　　　No me obligue
　　　　　vuestra Majestad, señor,　　　　　　　　　2115
　　　　　a que piense que imagine
　　　　　que yo he menester consuelos
　　　　　que mi opinión acrediten.
　　　　　¡Vive Dios!, que tengo esposa
　　　　　tan honesta, casta y firme,　　　　　　　　2120
　　　　　que deja atrás las romanas

your justice on your brother Enrique. Not because I know that his power offends my honour, sir, but for an honourable man, it's enough just to imagine an offense.

I look to you to save my honour's life. This way I'm curing it with prevention; to make it well I'm trying this method first. Because if in fact there were so fierce a malignance in the illness, I'd convoke a team of consultants on affronts, I'd lose all hope for my honour's life, I'd bathe it with blood, I'd bury it in the ground.

Don't worry; I only speak of blood from my own heart. Be assured that Prince Enrique is safe with me; and to this, let a witness speak: this dagger, this brilliant tongue of elegant steel, was his. You can see today that he's safe, because the Prince entrusts his dagger to me.

KING   Don Gutierre, it's all right; your brow is crowned with honour brighter than the sun's rays, be assured that your honour –

DON GUTIERRE   Your Majesty, sir, don't make me think that you imagine that I need reassurance that my reputation is in good standing. By God! I have a wife far more honest, chaste, and steadfast even

---

2095–8 I look to you … bury it in the ground [*tierra*]: Cruickshank (1989, pp. 174–5) notes that Gutierre adapts medical imagery for this portion of his speech: '**team of consultants on affronts** refers to *team of medical consultants*, "the consultation taken over the dangerously ill" (Covarrubias); to *los[e] all hope* is used in the sense of 'losing hope for something. Hopeless …, particularly the sick one, in whose health the physicians lack confidence" (Covarrubias); to **bathe … with blood** recalls the custom of washing the body of the deceased, and to bury in the ground [cover with earth], the burial'. (See also lines 2045–8 note.)
2101   *está = estad.*

	Lucrecia, Porcia, y Tomiris.	
	Ésta ha sido prevención	
	solamente.	
REY	Pues decidme;	
	para tantas prevenciones,	2125
	Gutierre, ¿qué es lo que visteis?	
DON GUTIERRE	Nada: que hombres como yo	
	no ven; basta que imaginen,	
	que sospechen, que prevengan,	
	que recelen, que adivinen,	2130
	que... no sé cómo lo diga;	
	que no hay voz que signifique	
	una cosa que no sea	
	un átomo indivisible.	
	Sólo a vuestra Majestad	2135
	di parte, para que evite	
	el daño que no hay; porque	
	si le hubiera, de mí fíe	
	que yo le diera el remedio	
	en vez, señor, de pedirle.	2140
REY	Pues ya que de vuestro honor	
	médico os llamáis, decidme,	
	don Gutierre, ¿qué remedios	
	antes del último hicisteis?	
DON GUTIERRE	No pedí a mi mujer celos,	2145
	y desde entonces la quise	
	más: vivía en una quinta	
	deleitosa y apacible;	
	y para que no estuviera	
	en las soledades triste,	2150
	truje a Sevilla mi casa,	
	y a vivir en ella vine,	
	adonde todo lo goza,	
	sin que nada a nadie envidie;	
	porque malos tratamientos	2155
	son para maridos viles	
	que pierden a sus agravios	
	el miedo, cuando los dicen.	
REY	El Infante viene allí,	
	y si aquí os ve, no es posible	2160
	que deje de conocer	
	las quejas que dél me disteis.	

	than Lucretia, Portia, and Tomyris. This is just for the sake of prevention.
KING	Then tell me: what did you see that requires so much prevention?
DON GUTIERRE	Nothing: men like me don't see; it's enough that they imagine, that they suspect, that they foresee, that they fear, that they deduce, that – I don't know how to say it; no word can fully signify a thing as small as an indivisible atom. I only confide in Your Majesty to prevent the injury that hasn't occurred yet; because if it had, you can be sure that I would have applied the remedy, sir, instead of asking you for it.
KING	Since you call yourself the physician of your honour, tell me, Don Gutierre, what remedies before the final one have you applied?
DON GUTIERRE	I didn't act jealous with my wife, and since then I've been even more loving. I used to live in a charming and peaceful country home; but to keep her from being sad in the solitude, I moved my household to Seville, where she has everything she could possibly desire. Abuse is for despicable husbands, who grow fond of their grievances when they put them into words.
KING	Here comes the Prince, and if he sees you, he'll know that you've come to me to complain.

2121–2   Lucretia, Portia, and Tomyris: Women famous for chastity, fidelity, and courage in the face of adversity. Cruickshank (1989, p. 176) points out that Tomyris was actually not Roman but a queen of the Massagetae.

2132–4   no word can fully signify ... an indivisible atom: That is, 'Words are too precise to express the ambiguity and complexity of honour' (Wardropper 1970, p. 602).

Mas acuérdome que un día
me dieron con voces tristes
quejas de vos, y yo entonces   2165
detrás de aquellos tapices
escondí a quien se quejaba;
y en el mismo caso pide
el daño el propio remedio,
pues al revés lo repite.   2170
Y así quiero hacer con vos
lo mismo que entonces hice;
pero con un orden más,
y es que nada aquí os obligue
a descubriros. Callad   2175
a cuanto viereis.

DON GUTIERRE   Humilde
estoy, señor, a tus pies.
Seré el pájaro que fingen
con una piedra en la boca.

Escóndese. Sale el Infante.

REY   Vengáis norabuena, Enrique,   2180
                aunque mala habrá de ser,
                pues me halláis...

DON ENRIQUE   ¡Ay de mí triste!

REY   ...enojado.

DON ENRIQUE   Pues, señor,
                ¿con quién lo estáis, que os obligue?

REY   Con vos, Infante, con vos.   2185

DON ENRIQUE   Será mi vida infelice:
                si enojado tengo al sol,
                veré mi mortal eclipse.

REY   ¿Vos, Enrique, no sabéis
                que más de un acero tiñe   2190
                el agravio en sangre real?

DON ENRIQUE   Pues ¿por quién, señor, lo dice
                vuestra Majestad?

REY   Por vos
                lo digo, por vos, Enrique.

But I recall that one day someone complained to me about you, and I sent the aggrieved party to hide behind those tapestries. The same circumstances would call for the same remedy, but here I'll reverse it. So this time, you go there, but with one more command: no matter what happens, don't come out. Whatever you hear, keep quiet.

DON GUTIERRE   I'm your humble servant, sir. My lips are sealed.

He hides. The Prince enters.

KING	Welcome, Enrique, although it will be ill come, because you find me –
PRINCE	Oh, no!
KING	– angry.
PRINCE	Well, sir, let me help. Why are you angry?
KING	It's because of you, Prince, it's you.
PRINCE	Then I'm truly unlucky. If I've angered the sun, a fatal eclipse is coming.
KING	Enrique, don't you know that an insult has stained more than one blade with royal blood?
PRINCE	Why do you tell me this, Your Majesty?
KING	Because of you, Enrique, because of you. Honour is a place

---

2168–70 The same circumstances ... I'll reverse it: Pedro refers to his having hidden Leonor in Act I after she made her complaint about Gutierre, and the latter approached. In fact, the structure of the King's speech in this matter is nearly identical to that of his speech in the first act. This remedy is 'reversed' because it is Gutierre who will be concealed.

2175–6 *Callad / a cuanto viereis* / **Whatever you hear, keep quiet:** The King actually says, 'Whatever you *see*'. Since Gutierre will be behind the tapestries, he will be unable to see anything that happens between the King and Enrique. See lines 921–2 note.

2178–9 *Seré el pájaro que fingen / con una piedra end la boca:* Literally, 'I'll be the bird they describe with a stone in its mouth'. According to Jones (p. 82), Gutierre may refer to the wild goose or crane. Jones cites an emblem book by J. Horozco y Covarrubias, published in 1589, which shows a bird in flight, with the motto *Silentium vita*, 'to be silent is to live'. The poem accompanying the emblem explains that the bird flies as silently as possible, carrying a stone in its mouth so that it will not cackle and give away its position to its predator, the royal eagle. For more on this image, see Cull, p. 116.

	El honor es reservado	2195
	lugar, donde el alma asiste;
	yo no soy Rey de las almas:
	harto en esto sólo os dije.
DON ENRIQUE	No os entiendo.
REY	Si a la enmienda
	vuestro amor no se apercibe,	2200
	dejando vanos intentos
	de bellezas imposibles,
	donde el alma de un vasallo
	con ley soberana vive,
	podrá ser de mi justicia	2205
	aun mi sangre no se libre.
DON ENRIQUE	Señor, aunque tu preceto
	es ley que tu lengua imprime
	en mi corazón, y en él
	como en el bronce se escribe,	2210
	escucha disculpas mías;
	que no será bien que olvides
	que con iguales orejas
	ambas partes han de oírse.
	Yo, señor, quise a una dama	2215
	(que ya sé por quién lo dices,
	si bien con poca ocasión);
	en efeto, yo la quise
	tanto…
REY	¿Qué importa, si ella
	es beldad tan imposible?	2220
DON ENRIQUE	Es verdad, pero…
REY	Callad.
DON ENRIQUE	Pues, señor, ¿no me permites
	disculparme?
REY	No hay disculpa;
	que es belleza que no admite
	objeción.
DON ENRIQUE	Es cierto, pero	2225
	el tiempo todo lo rinde,
	el amor todo lo puede.
REY	([*Ap.*] ¡Válgame Dios, qué mal hice
	en esconder a Gutierre!)
	Callad, callad.

	apart, where the soul abides. I am not the king of souls.
	Enough said.
PRINCE	I don't understand you.
KING	You must abandon your love. You've got to stop your hopeless pursuit of an impossible beauty, where the soul of a vassal reigns supreme. Otherwise, it could be that even one of my own flesh and blood will know the rigor of my justice.
PRINCE	Sir, although your command is a law imprinted on my heart and inscribed as if in bronze, listen to my explanation. It wouldn't be right for you to forget that both sides should be heard equally.
	I, sir, loved a lady (now I know whom you mean, although the criticism is unfair); the truth is, I loved her so much –
KING	What difference does it make, if this beauty is beyond your reach?
PRINCE	It's true, but –
KING	Be quiet.
PRINCE	But, sir, won't you let me explain?
KING	There is no explanation; this lady is beyond reproach.
PRINCE	It's true, but time conquers all; love has the power.
KING	([*Aside*] God help me; what a mistake it was to hide Gutierre!) Be quiet, be quiet!

2195–6 *El honor es reservado / lugar, donde el alma asiste* / **Honour is a place apart, where the soul abides:** King Pedro's remark recalls the peasant Pedro Crespo's widely noted speech in Calderón's *The Mayor of Zalamea* (*El alcalde de Zalamea*), lines 873–6: 'One must give one's property and life to the King; but honour is patrimony of the soul, and the soul belongs to God alone' (*Al Rey la hacienda y la vida / se ha de dar; pero el honor / es patrimonio del alma, / y el alma sólo es de Dios*).
2218 *efeto: efecto.*

DON ENRIQUE	No te incites	2230
	tanto contra mí, ignorando	
	la causa que a esto me obligue.	
REY	Yo lo sé todo muy bien.	
	([*Ap.*] ¡O qué lance tan terrible!)	
DON ENRIQUE	Pues yo, señor, he de hablar:	2235
	en fin, doncella la quise.	
	¿Quién, decid, agravió a quién?	
	¿Yo a un vasallo…	
DON GUTIERRE	[*Ap.*] ¡Ay infelice!	
DON ENRIQUE	…que antes que fuese su esposa	
	fue…?	
REY	No tenéis qué decirme.	2240
	Callad, callad, que ya sé	
	que por disculpa fingisteis	
	tal quimera. Infante, Infante,	
	vamos mediando los fines:	
	¿conocéis aquesta daga?	2245
DON ENRIQUE	Sin ella a palacio vine	
	una noche.	
REY	¿Y no sabéis	
	dónde la daga perdisteis?	
DON ENRIQUE	No, señor.	
REY	Yo sí, pues fue	
	adonde fuera posible	2250
	mancharse con sangre vuestra,	
	a no ser el que la rige	
	tan noble y leal vasallo.	
	¿No veis que venganza pide	
	el hombre que aun ofendido,	2255
	el pecho y las armas rinde?	
	¿Veis este puñal dorado?	
	Geroglífico es que dice	
	vuestro delito; a quejarse	
	viene de vos; yo he de oírle.	2260
	Tomad su acero, y en él	
	os mirad: veréis, Enrique,	
	vuestros defetos.	
DON ENRIQUE	Señor,	
	considera que me riñes	
	tan severo, que turbado…	2265

PRINCE	Don't be so upset, without knowing my side of the story.
KING	I know it all too well. ([*Aside*] Oh, what a terrible turn of events!)
PRINCE	Well, sir, I must speak: you see, I loved her when she was a maiden. So tell me, who offended whom? Did I harm a vassal –
DON GUTIERRE	[*Aside*] Oh, my God!
PRINCE	– if before she was his wife, she was – ?
KING	You can tell me nothing. Be quiet, be quiet! I know you've made up this monstrous fantasy as an excuse. Prince, Prince, let's get to the point: do you recognize this dagger?
PRINCE	One night I came back to the palace without it.
KING	And don't you know where you lost the dagger?
PRINCE	No, sir.
KING	Well, I do, because you left it where it could be stained with your own blood, if the man who surrendered it to me weren't such a noble and loyal vassal. Don't you see that although he was offended, the man has given me his heart and his weapons? He's asking for revenge. Do you see this golden dagger? It's a hieroglyph that spells out your crime; it comes to lodge a complaint against you; and I am bound to hear it. Take this blade, and look at yourself in it: Enrique, you'll see your imperfections.
PRINCE	Sir, you reproach me so harshly that I'm stunned –

REY   Tomad la daga…

Dale la daga, y al tomarla, turbado, el Infante corta al Rey la mano.

                  ¿Qué hiciste,
traidor?

DON ENRIQUE   ¿Yo?
REY   ¿Desta manera
tu acero en mi sangre tiñes?
¿Tú la daga que te di
hoy contra mi pecho esgrimes?   2270
¿Tú me quieres dar la muerte?
DON ENRIQUE   Mira, señor, lo que dices;
que yo turbado…
REY   ¿Tú a mí
te atreves? ¡Enrique, Enrique!
Detén el puñal, ya muero.   2275
DON ENRIQUE   ¿Hay confusiones más tristes?

Cáesele la daga al Infante.

                  Mejor es volver la espalda,
y aun ausentarme y partirme
donde en mi vida te vea,
porque de mí no imagines   2280
que puedo verter tu sangre
yo, mil veces infelice.

Vase.

REY   ¡Válgame el cielo! ¿Qué es esto?
¡Ah, qué aprehensión insufrible!
Bañado me vi en mi sangre;   2285
muerto estuve. ¿Qué infelice
imaginación me cerca,
que con espantos horribles
y con helados temores
el pecho y el alma oprime?   2290
Ruego a Dios que estos principios
no lleguen a tales fines,
que con diluvios de sangre
el mundo se escandalice.

Vase por otra puerta y sale don Gutierre.

KING   Take the dagger –

He gives him the dagger. The Prince is so distraught that, as he takes it, he cuts the King's hand.

                  What have you done, traitor?
PRINCE   I?
KING   You stain your blade with my blood like this? The dagger that I
                  gave you, now you turn it against me? Do you want to kill me?
PRINCE   Sir, think what you're saying – I was upset –
KING   You dare to raise your hand against me? Enrique, Enrique! Put
                  the knife down; I'm already dying.
PRINCE   Can there be a sadder misunderstanding than this?

The Prince drops the dagger.

                  It's better for me to turn my back, and go far away where I'll
                  never see you again, so that you won't imagine of me that I
                  could spill your blood. I'm so unhappy.

He leaves.

KING   Heaven help me! What is this? Ah, what an unbearable
                  premonition! I saw myself bathed in my own blood; I was dead.
                  What unhappy fantasy besieges me, weighing down my heart
                  with horrible dread and icy fear? God, I beg of you, please don't
                  let this beginning come to that end, scandalizing the world with
                  a deluge of blood.

He leaves through a different door and Don Gutierre enters.

2283–94 Heaven help me! … deluge of blood: King Pedro has a premonition of his death. In the year 1369 the historical king was in fact stabbed to death by Prince Enrique during civil war at the Montiel battlefield. See 'Historical Contexts and Responses' in Introduction.

DON GUTIERRE Todo es prodigios el día.   2295
        Con asombros tan terribles,
        de que yo estaba escondido
        no es mucho que el Rey se olvide.
        ¡Válgame Dios! ¿Qué escuché?
        Mas ¿para qué lo repite   2300
        la lengua, cuando mi agravio
        con mi desdicha se mide?
        Arranquemos de una vez
        de tanto mal las raíces.
        Muera Mencía; su sangre   2305
        bañe el lecho donde asiste:
        y pues aqueste puñal

Levántale.

        hoy segunda vez me rinde
        el Infante, con él muera.
        Mas no es bien que lo publique;   2310
        porque si sé que el secreto
        altas vitorias consigue,
        y que agravio que es oculto
        oculta venganza pide,
        muera Mencía de suerte   2315
        que ninguno lo imagine.
        Pero antes que llegue a esto,
        la vida el cielo me quite,
        porque no vea tragedias
        de un amor tan infelice.   2320
        ¿Para cuándo, para cuándo
        esos azules viriles
        guardan un rayo? ¿No es tiempo
        de que sus puntas se vibren,
        preciando de tan piadosos?   2325
        ¿No hay, claros cielos, decidme,
        para un desdichado muerte?
        ¿No hay un rayo para un triste?

Vase. Salen doña Mencía y Jacinta.

JACINTA   Señora, ¿qué tristeza
        turba la admiración a tu belleza,   2330
        que la noche y el día
        no haces sino llorar?

DON GUTIERRE   This day is filled with monstrous events. With such terrible revelations, no wonder the King forgot I was hidden. God help me! What did I hear? But why put it into words, when my misery expresses the magnitude of my injury?

      With a single act let us tear out the roots of so much evil. Let Mencía die; let her blood bathe the bed where she lies: and since today the Prince surrenders his dagger to me for the second time,

He picks it up.

let her die by it. But no one must find out what's happened. I know that secrecy wins great victories, and since a hidden offence requires a hidden revenge, let Mencía die in a way that no one guesses the truth.

      But before I do this, may heaven take my life, may it keep me from playing out the tragedy of such an unhappy love. Why, why do those charged blue skies not streak with a bolt of lightning? Isn't now the time for their sharp points to flash, if they're so attuned to my misery? Clear blue skies, tell me, why don't you cast down a lightning bolt to strike me dead? Why don't you take pity on a man as sad as I?

He leaves.

[* *]*

Doña Mencía and Jacinta enter.

JACINTA   Madam, what sadness plagues you? Day and night you do nothing but weep.

2311–4 I know that secrecy wins great victories, and since a hidden offence requires a hidden revenge: Gutierre articulates a principle informing all three of Calderón's honour plays, and forming the title of one of them: *A secreto agravio, secreta venganza* (*Secret Wrong, Secret Revenge*). The third honour play is *El pintor de su deshonra* (*The Painter of His Dishonour*). See 'The *Drama de Honor*' in Introduction.

DOÑA MENCÍA	La pena mía

no se rinde a razones.
En una confusión de confusiones,
ni medidas, ni cuerdas,   2335
desde la noche triste, si te acuerdas,
que viviendo en la quinta,
te dije que conmigo había, Jacinta,
hablado don Enrique
(no sé cómo mi mal te signifique),   2340
y tú después dijiste que no era
posible, porque afuera,
a aquella misma hora que yo digo,
el Infante también habló contigo,
estoy triste y dudosa,   2345
confusa, divertida y temerosa,
pensando que no fuese
Gutierre quien conmigo habló.

JACINTA   ¿Pues ése
es engaño que pudo
suceder?

DOÑA MENCÍA   Sí, Jacinta, que no dudo   2350
que de noche, y hablando
quedo, y yo tan turbada, imaginando
en él mismo, venía;
bien tal engaño suceder podía.
Con esto el verle agora   2355
conmigo alegre, y que consigo llora
(porque al fin los enojos,
que son grandes amigos de los ojos,
no les encubren nada),
me tiene en tantas penas anegada.   2360

Sale Coquín.

COQUÍN   Señora.
DOÑA MENCÍA   ¿Qué hay de nuevo?
COQUÍN   Apenas a contártelo me atrevo:
don Enrique el Infante…
DOÑA MENCÍA   Tente, Coquín, no pases adelante;
que su nombre, no más, me causa espanto;   2365
tanto le temo, o le aborrezco tanto.
COQUÍN   No es de amor el suceso,
y por eso lo digo.

DA. MENCÍA	My pain is too great for words. Since one crazy, immeasurable confusion out of many on that sad night – I don't know how to explain my malady to you, Jacinta. You remember that night, when we lived in the country, when I told you I'd spoken with Enrique, and you said it was impossible, because he'd been talking to you at the same time outside? Since then I've been sad and full of doubts, bewildered, preoccupied, afraid, thinking that it may actually have been Gutierre who spoke with me.
JACINTA	Could that have happened?
DA. MENCÍA	Yes, Jacinta. I'm sure that at night, when I was so upset imagining he'd come, perhaps he did, speaking in a low voice. Yes, it could certainly have happened. So now, seeing him acting happy with me, but weeping to himself (because worries are drawn to the eyes, and will always show themselves eventually), I feel like I'm drowning in a sea of pain.

Coquín enters.

COQUÍN	Madam!
DA. MENCÍA	What is it?
COQUÍN	I hardly dare tell you. Don Enrique, the Prince –
DA. MENCÍA	Stop, Coquín, don't go on. Just the sound of his name fills me with dread, I'm so afraid of him, I abhor him.
COQUÍN	What's happened isn't about love, so let me tell you.

DOÑA MENCÍA   Y yo por eso
    lo escucharé.
COQUÍN   El Infante,
    que fue, señora, tu imposible amante,   2370
    con don Pedro su hermano
    hoy un lance ha tenido (pero en vano
    contártelo pretendo,
    por no saberle bien, o porque entiendo
    que no son justas leyes   2375
    que hombres de burlas hablen de los reyes):
    esto aparte, en efeto,
    Enrique me llamó, y con gran secreto
    dijo: 'A doña Mencía
    este recado da de parte mía: 2380
    que su desdén tirano
    me ha quitado la gracia de mi hermano,
    y huyendo desta tierra,
    hoy a la ajena patria me destierra,
    donde vivir no espero,   2385
    pues de Mencía aborrecido muero'.
DOÑA MENCÍA   ¿Por mí el Infante ausente,
    sin la gracia del Rey? ¡Cosa que intente
    con novedad tan grande,
    que mi opinión en voz del vulgo ande!   2390
    ¿Qué haré, cielos?
JACINTA   Agora
    el remedio mejor será, señora,
    prevenir este daño.
COQUÍN   ¿Cómo puede?
JACINTA   Rogándole al Infante que se quede;
    pues si una vez se ausenta,   2395
    como dicen, por ti, será tu afrenta
    pública, que no es cosa
    la ausencia de un infante tan dudosa
    que no se diga luego
    cómo, y por qué.
COQUÍN   ¿Pues cuándo oirá ese ruego,   2400
    si, calzada la espuela,
    ya en su imaginación Enrique vuela?
JACINTA   Escribiéndole agora
    un papel, en que diga mi señora

DA. MENCÍA	In that case, I'll listen.
COQUÍN	The Prince, who pursued you with his impossible love, has had a quarrel with his brother Don Pedro today (but I'm in no position to tell you this, because I'm not sure of the details, and I know it's wrong for a man of folly to speak of kings).
	Anyway, Enrique summoned me in great secrecy, and said, 'Take this message to Doña Mencía for me: tell her that her cruel disdain has caused me to lose my brother's favour, and today he exiles me to a foreign land, where I don't expect to live, because, if Mencía abhors me, I'll die'.
DA. MENCÍA	Because of me – the Prince – gone – without the King's favour? Does he want to cause a scandal, making my name fodder for gossip? Heavens, what can I do?
JACINTA	Madam, prevention is the best remedy.
DA. MENCÍA	How?
JACINTA	Ask the Prince to stay: once they say he's gone because of you, your disgrace will be public, and the departure of a Prince under such murky circumstances will cause all sorts of questions about what happened.
COQUÍN	But how will he hear her plea, if he's already buckling on his spurs to go?
JACINTA	She can write him a note right now, saying he mustn't leave, for

---

2376   a man of folly, or fool (*hombre de burlas*) 'is the man who has little wisdom and maturity in his behaviour, and is reputed to be useless in matters of consequence' (*Autoridades*, I, p. 717b). See also lines 2730–3.

2388   *Cosa que*: See line 1283 note.

2392–3 Madame, prevention is the best remedy: See line 1243, and line 1467 notes.

	que a su opinión conviene	2405
	que no se ausente; pues para eso tiene	
	lugar, si tú le llevas.	
DOÑA MENCÍA	Pruebas de honor son peligrosas pruebas;	
	pero con todo quiero	
	escribir el papel, pues considero,	2410
	y no con necio engaño,	
	que es de dos daños éste el menor daño,	
	si hay menor en los daños que recibo.	
	Quedaos aquí los dos mientras yo escribo.	

Vase.

JACINTA	¿Qué tienes estos días,	2415
	Coquín, que andas tan triste? ¿No solías	
	ser alegre? ¿Qué efeto	
	te tiene así?	
COQUÍN	Metíme a ser discreto	
	por mi mal, y hame dado	
	tan grande hipocondría en este lado	2420
	que me muero.	
JACINTA	¿Y qué es hipocondría?	
COQUÍN	Es una enfermedad que no la había	
	habrá dos años, ni en el mundo era.	
	Usóse poco ha, y de manera	
	lo que se usa, amiga, no se excusa,	2425
	que una dama, sabiendo que se usa,	
	le dijo a su galán muy triste un día:	
	'tráigame un poco uced de hipocondría'.	
	Mas señor entra agora.	
JACINTA	¡Ay Dios! Voy a avisar a mi señora.	2430

Sale don Gutierre.

DON GUTIERRE	Tente, Jacinta, espera.	
	¿Dónde corriendo vas desa manera?	
JACINTA	Avisar pretendía	
	a mi señora de que ya venía	
	tu persona.	
DON GUTIERRE	([*Ap.*] ¡O criados!,	2435
	en efeto, enemigos no excusados;	
	turbados de temor los dos se han puesto.)	
	Ven acá, dime tú lo que hay en esto;	
	dime, ¿por qué corrías?	

	the sake of her reputation: there's time for that, if you take it to him.
DA. MENCÍA	This test of my honour is so dangerous. But I'll write the letter, because all things considered, I think it will be the lesser of two evils – if any of the evils that come my way can be any less than the others. The two of you stay here while I write.

She leaves.

JACINTA	What's the matter these days, Coquín? You seem so sad. Didn't you used to be happy? What's making you act like this?
COQUÍN	I foolishly set out to be discreet, and it's given me such a big hypochondria in the side that I'm dying.
JACINTA	What's a hypochondria?
COQUÍN	It's a disease that didn't exist until two years ago, and now everybody wants to have it. One lady, knowing it was the latest fad, said very sadly to her boyfriend one day, 'bring me a little hypochondria, if you please'.
	But here comes our master.
JACINTA	Dear God! I'll go tell my mistress.

Don Gutierre enters.

DON GUTIERRE	Stop, Jacinta, wait. Why are you running off like that?
JACINTA	I was going to tell my lady you're coming.
DON GUTIERRE	([*Aside*] Oh, servants, enemies living in our very midst. The two of them have begun to shake with fear.) Come here and tell me what's going on. Tell me, why were you running?

2420–8 such a big hypochondria … '… if you please': 'Coquín refers here to a melancholy malady thought [during Calderón's time] to be caused by a malfunction in one of the abdominal organs known as the "hypochondria" or "hypochondrias". These were believed to absorb and filter excess melancholy from the body. An interruption of the process, however, could trap heated melancholy in one's system and cause him pain in the side – Coquín's complaint' (Soufas 1982, p. 205). See also Soufas 1990, pp. 96–9. Cruickshank (1989, pp.189–90) hypothesizes that Calderón has Coquín use the word in its modern sense of imaginary illness.

JACINTA	Sólo por avisar de que venías,	2440
	señor, a mi señora.	
DON GUTIERRE	([*Ap.*] Los labios sella.	
	Mas déste lo sabré mejor que della.)	
	Coquín, tú me has servido	
	noble siempre, en mi casa te has criado:	
	a ti vuelvo rendido;	2445
	dime, dime por Dios lo que ha pasado.	
COQUÍN	Señor, si algo supiera,	
	de lástima no más te lo dijera.	
	¡Plegue a Dios, mi señor...!	
DON GUTIERRE	¡No, no des voces!	
	Di ¿a qué aquí te turbaste?	2450
COQUÍN	Somos de buen turbar; mas esto baste.	
DON GUTIERRE	([*Ap.*] Señas los dos se han hecho.	
	Ya no son cobardías de provecho.)	
	Idos de aquí los dos.	

Vanse.

Solos estamos,
honor, lleguemos ya; desdicha, vamos.   2455
¿Quién vio en tantos enojos
matar las manos, y llorar los ojos?

Descubre a doña Mencía escribiendo.

Escribiendo Mencía
está; ya es fuerza ver lo que escribía.

Quítale el papel.

DOÑA MENCÍA	¡Ay Dios! ¡Válgame el cielo!	2460

Ella se desmaya.

DON GUTIERRE	Estatua viva se quedó de hielo.

Lee.

'Vuestra Alteza, señor... (¡Que por Alteza
vino mi honor a dar a tal bajeza!)
no se ausente...' Deténte,
voz; pues le ruega aquí que no se ausente,   2465
a tanto mal me ofrezco,
que casi las desdichas me agradezco.

JACINTA	Just to let my lady know that you were coming, sir.
DON GUTIERRE	([*Aside*] Her lips are sealed. But I'll learn more from this one than from her.) Coquín, you've always served me nobly; you were raised in my home. I'm at your mercy: tell me, for God's sake, tell me what's happened.
COQUÍN	Sir, if I knew anything, out of pity I'd tell you. Good heavens, sir – !
DON GUTIERRE	No, don't shout! Tell me, what upset you just now?
COQUÍN	We're highly upsettable, that's all.
DON GUTIERRE	([*Aside*] They're signalling each other. Their fussing isn't doing me any good.) The two of you, leave.

They leave.

> Now that we're alone, honour, let's go in. Misfortune, come with me. Who would ever imagine that misfortunes could drive a man's eyes to weep as his hands took a life?

He discovers Doña Mencía writing.

> Mencía's writing; I have to see what it is.

He takes the paper from her.

DA. MENCÍA	Oh, God! Heaven help me!

She faints.

DON GUTIERRE	She's become a living sculpture of ice.

He reads.

> 'Your Highness, sir' – to think that his Highness brought my honour so low! – 'don't go away – ' Stop, voice! She begs him not to leave. Now I surrender myself to such unspeakable evil

---

2443–4 you were raised in my home: This statement contradicts Coquín's own version of his life that he gave the King in Act I. See lines 750–3, and Introduction, note 17.
2457+ *He discovers Doña Mencía writing*: Here Don Gutierre may open the center curtain to reveal Mencía writing. See notes to lines 1896+ and 2871+.

¿Si aquí le doy la muerte?
Mas esto ha de pensarse de otra suerte.
Despediré criadas y criados;   2470
solos han de quedarse mis cuidados
conmigo; y ya que ha sido
Mencía la mujer que yo he querido

Escribe don Gutierre.

más en mi vida, quiero
que en el último vale, en el postrero   2475
parasismo, me deba
la más nueva piedad, la acción más nueva;
ya que la cura he de aplicar postrera,
no muera el alma, aunque la vida muera.

Vase. Va volviendo en sí doña Mencía.

DOÑA MENCÍA   Señor, detén la espada,   2480
no me juzgues culpada:
el cielo sabe que inocente muero.
¿Qué fiera mano, qué sangriento acero
en mi pecho ejecutas? ¡Tente, tente!
Una mujer no mates inocente.   2485
Mas, ¿qué es esto? ¡Ay de mí! ¿No estaba agora
Gutierre aquí? ¿No vía (¿quién lo ignora?)
que en mi sangre bañada
moría, en rubias ondas anegada?
¡Ay Dios, este desmayo   2490
fue de mi vida aquí mortal ensayo!
¡Qué ilusión! Por verdad lo dudo y creo.
El papel romperé... ¿Pero qué veo?
De mi esposo es la letra, y desta suerte
la sentencia me intima de mi muerte.   2495

Lee.

'El amor te adora, el honor te aborrece; y así el uno te mata, y
el otro te avisa: dos horas tienes de vida; cristiana eres, salva el
alma, que la vida es imposible'.

¡Válgame Dios! ¡Jacinta, hola! ¿Qué es esto?
¿Nadie responde? ¡Otro temor funesto!
¿No hay ninguna criada?
Mas, ¡ay de mí!, la puerta está cerrada:
nadie en casa me escucha.   2500

that I welcome all challenges. Shall I kill her here? But I have to think this through. I'll send the servants away; only my worries will stay behind with me. Since Mencía is the woman I've loved most –

Don Gutierre writes.

– in my life, in her last farewell, in her final breath, I want her indebted to me for the most supreme mercy, the most exceptional gesture. Although I'm going to apply the final cure, although Mencía will die, may her soul live on.

He leaves. Mencía begins to regain consciousness.

DA. MENCÍA Sir, put down your sword, don't judge me guilty; heaven knows I die innocent. What beastly hand is this, thrusting the bloody steel into my heart? Stop, stop! Don't kill an innocent woman.

But what's this? Ah, me! Wasn't Gutierre just here? Didn't I just see myself bathed in blood? I'm sure of it – I was dying, drowning in waves of crimson. Oh, God, this swoon was a rehearsal of my death! What an illusion! I doubt it, and I believe it at the same time. I'll tear up the letter – but what's this? It's my husband's handwriting, and this is how he reveals to me my death sentence.

She reads.

'My love adores you, my honour abhors you; and so the one will do away with you and the other gives you advice: you have two hours to live; you're a Christian; save your soul, because it's impossible to save your life'.

God help me! Jacinta, where are you? What's this? Nobody answers? What a deathly fear! Are no servants about? But, ah, me!, the door is locked; no one's home to hear me. What agony,

---

'My love adores you … to save your life': In Shakespeare's *Othello*, a play with some similarities to Calderón's honour dramas, the protagonist intends – but, overcome by jealousy, fails – to allow his wife Desdemona, who he does not realize is innocent, to ready herself spiritually before he kills her (V, ii).

Mucha es mi turbación, mi pena es mucha.
Destas ventanas son los hierros rejas,
y en vano a nadie le diré mis quejas,
que caen a unos jardines, donde apenas
habrá quien oiga repetidas penas.　　　　　　　　　2505
¿Dónde iré desta suerte,
tropezando en la sombra de mi muerte?

Vase. Salen el Rey y don Diego.

REY　　　　　　　En fin, ¿Enrique se fue?
DON DIEGO　　Sí, señor; aquesta tarde
　　　　　　　　salió de Sevilla.
REY　　　　　　　　　　　　Creo　　　　　　　　　2510
　　　　　　　　que ha presumido arrogante
　　　　　　　　que él solamente de mí
　　　　　　　　podrá en el mundo librarse.
　　　　　　　　¿Y dónde va?
DON DIEGO　　　　　　　Yo presumo
　　　　　　　　que a Consuegra.
REY　　　　　　　　　　　　Está el Infante　　　　2515
　　　　　　　　Maestre allí, y querrán los dos
　　　　　　　　a mis espaldas vengarse
　　　　　　　　de mí.
DON DIEGO　　　　Tus hermanos son,
　　　　　　　　y es forzoso que te amen
　　　　　　　　como a hermano, y como a Rey　　　2520
　　　　　　　　te adoren: dos naturales
　　　　　　　　obediencias son.
REY　　　　　　　　　　　　Y Enrique,
　　　　　　　　¿quién lleva que le acompañe?
DON DIEGO　　Don Arias.
REY　　　　　　　　　　Es su privanza.
DON DIEGO　　Música hay en esta calle.　　　　　2525
REY　　　　　　　Vámonos llegando a ellos;
　　　　　　　　quizá con lo que cantaren
　　　　　　　　me divertiré.
DON DIEGO　　　　　　La música
　　　　　　　　es antídoto a los males

Cantan.　　　　*El Infante don Enrique*　　　　　2530
　　　　　　　　hoy se despidió del Rey;

what panic! These windows are blocked by iron bars, and the gardens below are deserted. Where can I go like this, stumbling into the shadow of my death?

She leaves.

[* * *]

The King and Don Diego enter.

KING	So, Enrique's gone?
DON DIEGO	Yes, sir; he left Seville this afternoon.
KING	I think he arrogantly believes that he's the only one in the world who can escape me. And where is he going?
DON DIEGO	To Consuegra, I assume.
KING	The Prince Grand Master is there, and the two of them will conspire behind my back to take revenge against me.
DON DIEGO	They're your brothers: they must love you, and revere you as their king. These are two natural obligations.
KING	And Enrique, who goes with him?
DON DIEGO	Don Arias.
KING	Arias is his favourite.
DON DIEGO	There's music in this street.
KING	Let's go up to them; perhaps they'll sing something that will amuse me.
DON DIEGO	Music is an antidote to troubles.
MUSIC	*Today Prince Don Enrique*

2514–8 The Prince Grand Master … against me: Don Fadrique was Enrique's twin brother, whom Pedro eventually executed. For Calderón's audience, mention of Consuegra, a town in the central Spanish province of Toledo, would also strike an ominous note. It was near Consuegra, in the plain below the mountains of Montiel, that during civil war Prince Enrique was to murder King Pedro. See Calderón's ballad in lines 2634–7. Valbuena Briones (pp. 104–5) points out that Consuegra was the legendary site of national tragedies including the conspiracy of the treacherous don Julián for the Moors to invade Spain, and the death in battle of the Cid's son.

su pesadumbre y su ausencia
quiera Dios que pare en bien.

REY   ¡Qué triste voz! Vos, don Diego,
                     echad por aquesa calle,   2535
                     no se nos escape quien
                     canta desatinos tales.

Vase cada uno por su puerta, y salen don Gutierre y Ludovico, cubierto el rostro.

DON GUTIERRE   Entra, no tengas temor;
                     que ya es tiempo que destape
                     tu rostro, y encubra el mío.   2540
LUDOVICO   ¡Válgame Dios!
DON GUTIERRE   No te espante
                     nada que vieres.
LUDOVICO   Señor,
                     de mi casa me sacasteis
                     esta noche; pero apenas
                     me tuvisteis en la calle,   2545
                     cuando un puñal me pusisteis
                     al pecho, sin que cobarde
                     vuestro intento resistiese,
                     que fue cubrirme y taparme
                     el rostro, y darme mil vueltas   2550
                     luego a mis propios umbrales.
                     Dijisteis más, que mi vida
                     estaba en no destaparme;
                     un hora he andado con vos,
                     sin saber por dónde ande.   2555
                     Y con ser la admiración
                     de aqueste caso tan grave,
                     más me turba y me suspende
                     impensadamente hallarme
                     en una casa tan rica,   2560
                     sin ver que la habite nadie
                     sino vos, habiéndoos visto
                     siempre ese embozo delante.
                     ¿Qué me queréis?
DON GUTIERRE   Que te esperes
                     aquí sólo un breve instante.   2565

Vase.

> *from King Pedro took his leave;*
> *God grant a good conclusion*
> *to his absence and his grief.*

KING   What a sad voice! Don Diego, you go down that street. Don't let
            the one singing such nonsense get away.

Each leaves through a different door.

[* *]*

Don Gutierre enters with Ludovico, whose face is covered.

DON GUTIERRE Go in, don't be afraid. Now it's time for you to uncover your
              face, and for me to conceal mine.
LUDOVICO   God help me!
DON GUTIERRE Don't be shocked by anything you see.
LUDOVICO   Sir, you took me from my house tonight, but as soon as you had
              me in the street, you put a dagger to my chest. I was afraid, so
              I didn't resist when you blindfolded me, and then outside my
              own door you spun me around a thousand times. You told me
              that my life depended on remaining blindfolded. I've walked
              an hour with you, without knowing where we're going. And
              to top my astonishment at all that's happened, I'm even more
              disturbed and upset to find myself at such a wealthy house,
              without seeing that anyone other than you dwells in it, and only
              having seen you covered up like that. What do you want from
              me?
DON GUTIERRE Wait here for just a minute.

He leaves.

2554   ***un hora*** = *una hora*: the apocopation can be used in poetry to preserve the metre.

LUDOVICO	¿Qué confusiones son éstas,
	que a tal extremo me traen?
	¡Válgame Dios!

Vuelve [don Gutierre].

DON GUTIERRE	Tiempo es ya	
	de que entres aquí; mas antes	
	escúchame: aqueste acero	2570
	será de tu pecho esmalte,	
	si resistes lo que yo	
	tengo agora de mandarte.	
	Asómate a ese aposento.	
	¿Qué ves en él?	
LUDOVICO	Una imagen	2575
	de la muerte, un bulto veo,	
	que sobre una cama yace;	
	dos velas tiene a los lados,	
	y un crucifijo delante.	
	Quién es no puedo decir,	2580
	que con unos tafetanes	
	el rostro tiene cubierto.	
DON GUTIERRE	Pues a ese vivo cadáver	
	que ves, has de dar la muerte.	
LUDOVICO	Pues ¿qué quieres?	
DON GUTIERRE	Que la sangres,	2585
	y la dejes, que rendida	
	a su violencia desmaye	
	la fuerza, y que en tanto horror	
	tú atrevido la acompañes,	
	hasta que por breve herida	2590
	ella expire y se desangre.	
	No tienes a qué apelar,	
	si buscas en mí piedades,	
	sino obedecer, si quieres	
	vivir.	
LUDOVICO	Señor, tan cobarde	2595
	te escucho, que no podré	
	obedecerte.	
DON GUTIERRE	Quien hace	
	por consejos rigurosos	
	mayores temeridades,	

LUDOVICO   What bewildering events are these, that bring me to such a pass?
                 God help me!

He [Don Gutierre] returns.

DON GUTIERRE Now it's time for you to come in here, but first, listen: if you
              don't do what I say, you'll find this blade in your heart. Look in
              that room. What do you see there?
LUDOVICO   An image of death. I see a figure lying on a bed, with a candle
              on either side, and a crucifix before it. I can't say who it is,
              because the face is veiled in silk.
DON GUTIERRE Well, to that living corpse you are going to deliver death.
LUDOVICO   What are you asking me to do?
DON GUTIERRE Bleed her, and continue the bleeding until, overcome by its
              violence, her strength fades. You'll remain with her in this
              horror until, from the briefest cut, she bleeds to death. There's
              no point in appealing to me for mercy. If you want to live, do
              it.
LUDOVICO   Sir, I'm so afraid, I won't be able to.
DON GUTIERRE One whose honour demands of him greater feats of daring will

---

2585 Bleed her: During Calderón's time, bloodletting, commonly performed by barbers,
was a course of treatment for some maladies.

	darte la muerte sabrá.	2600
LUDOVICO	Fuerza es que mi vida guarde.	
DON GUTIERRE	Y haces bien, porque en el mundo	

ya hay quien viva porque mate.
Desde aquí te estoy mirando,
Ludovico: entra delante.   2605

Vase [Ludovico].

Éste fue el más fuerte medio
para que mi afrenta acabe
disimulada, supuesto
que el veneno fuera fácil
de averiguar, las heridas   2610
imposibles de ocultarse.
Y así, constando la muerte,
y diciendo que fue lance
forzoso hacer la sangría,
ninguno podrá probarme   2615
lo contrario, si es posible
que una venda se desate.
Haber traído a este hombre
con recato semejante,
fue bien; pues si descubierto   2620
viniera, y viera sangrarse
una mujer, y por fuerza,
fuera presunción notable.
Éste no podrá decir,
cuando cuente aqueste trance,   2625
quién fue la mujer; demás
que, cuando de aquí le saque,
muy lejos ya de mi casa,
estoy dispuesto a matarle.
Médico soy de mi honor,   2630
la vida pretendo darle
con una sangría; que todos
curan a costa de sangre.

Vase, y vuelven el Rey, y don Diego, cada uno por su puerta; y cantan dentro.

MÚSICA	*Para Consuegra camina,*	
	donde piensa que han de ser	2635
	teatros de mil tragedias	
	las montañas de Montiel.	

have no trouble killing you.

LUDOVICO   I've got to save myself.

DON GUTIERRE   And well you should, because some people live in order to kill. I'm watching you from here, Ludovico: go in.

He [Ludovico] leaves.

This was the surest way to get rid of my affront secretly, given that poison would be easy to detect, and a wound impossible to hide. And so, when the death becomes known, if I say the bleeding was necessary, no one will be able to prove any differently: it's always possible for a bandage to come loose. I was right to bring the man here with this precaution. If he'd been able to tell where we were going, and saw himself forced to bleed a woman, my guilt would have been clear. When this man tells about the death, he won't be able to say who the woman was. Besides, when I take him from here, when we're far away from my house, I'm prepared to kill him. I've been the physician of my honour. I've saved its life by bleeding – after all, everyone cures with a flow of blood.

He leaves.

[* *]*

The King and Don Diego return through different doors, and there is singing within.

MUSIC   *He rides toward Consuegra,*
thinking there he'll see
Montiel Peaks made theatres
for a thousand tragedies.

2603   *hay quien viva porque mate* / **some people live in order to kill:** 'The subjunctive *viva* can be accounted for by the presence of an indefinite antecedent; *mate* is dependent upon *porque* which is here equivalent to *para que*' (Jones, p. 99).

REY	Don Diego.
DON DIEGO	Señor.
REY	Supuesto

que cantan en esta calle,
¿no hemos de saber quién es?   2640
¿Habla por ventura el aire?

DON DIEGO   No te desvele, señor,
oír estas necedades,
porque a vuestro enojo ya
versos en Sevilla se hacen.   2645
Dos hombres vienen aquí.

REY   Es verdad: no hay que esperarles
respuesta. Hoy el conocerles
me importa.

Saca don Gutierre a Ludovico, tapado el rostro.

DON GUTIERRE [*Ap.*]   ¡Que así me ataje
el cielo, que con la muerte   2650
deste hombre eche otra llave
al secreto! Ya me es fuerza
de aquestos dos retirarme;
que nada me está peor
que conocerme en tal parte.   2655
Dejaréle en este puesto.

[Vase.]

DON DIEGO   De los dos, señor, que antes
venían, se volvió el uno,
y el otro se quedó.

REY   A darme
confusión; que si le veo   2660
a la poca luz que esparce
la luna, no tiene forma
su rostro: confusa imagen
el bulto mal acabado
parece de un blanco jaspe.   2665

DON DIEGO   Téngase su Majestad,
que yo llegaré.

REY   Dejadme,
don Diego. ¿Quién eres, hombre?

LUDOVICO   Dos confusiones son parte,

KING	Don Diego.
DON DIEGO	Sir.
KING	If they're singing in this street, can't we find out who they are? Could it possibly be the whistling of the wind?
DON DIEGO	Don't lose sleep over these foolish stunts, sir, they make up songs in Seville just to vex you. Two men are approaching.
KING	Yes, let's not wait for them to reach us. I've got to know who they are.

Don Gutierre emerges with Ludovico, who is blindfolded.

DON GUTIERRE	[*Aside*] Ah, now I can't throw away the key to my secret by killing this man! I have to get away from those two; nothing would be worse for me than to be recognized under such circumstances. I'll leave him here.

He leaves.

DON DIEGO	One of the two men turned away, and left the other behind.
KING	To confound me, because I can see him in the faint moonlight, but his face has no shape. The ill-formed figure resembles an unfinished sculpture.
DON DIEGO	Your Majesty, stay here. I'll go up to him.
KING	Let me, Don Diego. Who are you, man?
LUDOVICO	I'm too confused to answer you, sir.

2646 Two men are approaching: While all previous editions assign this observation to the King and the following speech to Don Diego, the reverse attributions better suit the characters.

señor, a no responderos: 2670
la una, la humilidad que trae
consigo un pobre oficial,

Descúbrese.

para que con reyes hable
(que ya os conocí en la voz,
luz que tan notorio os hace);   2675
la otra, la novedad
del suceso más notable
que el vulgo, archivo confuso,
califica en sus anales.

REY   ¿Qué os ha sucedido?
LUDOVICO   A vos   2680
lo diré; escuchadme aparte.

REY   Retiraos allí, don Diego.
DON DIEGO   [*Ap.*] Sucesos son admirables
cuantos esta noche veo:
Dios con bien della me saque.   2685

LUDOVICO   No la vi el rostro, mas sólo
entre repetidos ayes
escuché: 'Inocente muero;
el cielo no te demande
mi muerte'. Esto dijo, y luego   2690
expiró; y en este instante
el hombre mató la luz,
y por los pasos que antes
entré, salí. Sintió ruido
al llegar a aquesta calle,   2695
y dejóme en ella solo.
Fáltame ahora de avisarte,
señor, que saqué bañadas
las manos en roja sangre,
y que fui por las paredes   2700
como que quise arrimarme,
manchando todas las puertas,
por si pueden las señales
descubrir la casa.

REY   Bien
hicisteis: venid a hablarme   2705
con lo que hubiereis sabido,

For one thing, I'm just a poor tradesman, too humble –

He takes off the blindfold.

	– to speak with kings (the sound of your voice is like a beacon that gives you away). Also, something strange has just happened, the most remarkable thing ever: rumours and ballads about it will live on people's tongues for a long time to come.
KING	What's happened to you?
LUDOVICO	I'll tell you; please listen to me in private.
KING	Go over there, Don Diego.
DON DIEGO	[*Aside*] Tonight I've seen so many astonishing things: may God bring me safely through it all.
LUDOVICO	I didn't see her face, I only heard her sighing, 'I die innocent: don't let heaven indict you for my death'. She said this, and then she died; and at that moment the man extinguished the light. He took me out of the house the same way he brought me in. When we came to this street he heard a noise and left me here alone. I must tell you now, sir, that I left with my hands bathed red with blood, and I went along the walls as if I needed to lean on them, marking all the doors, to show where the house can be found.
KING	You did well: come speak to me about everything you know,

2677–9 []*el suceso más notable ... califica en sus anales*: Literally, 'the most remarkable event to which the common people, confused archive that they are, will bear witness in their annals'. The annals of the common people would be the oral tradition, including rumours, ballads, proverbs, and legends.

2686　I didn't see her face: We do not hear the beginning of Ludovico's account to the King. Possibly Don Diego's aside is meant to be heard instead, sparing us from listening to details of which we are already aware.

	y tomad este diamante,	
	y decid que por las señas	
	dél os permitan hablarme	
	a cualquier hora que vais.	2710
LUDOVICO	El cielo, señor, os guarde.	

Vase.

REY	Vamos, don Diego.	
DON DIEGO	¿Qué es eso?	
REY	El suceso más notable	
	del mundo.	
DON DIEGO	Triste has quedado.	
REY	Forzoso ha sido asombrarme.	2715
DON DIEGO	Vente a acostar, que ya el día	
	entre dorados celajes	
	asoma.	
REY	No he de poder	
	sosegar, hasta que halle	
	una casa que deseo.	2720
DON DIEGO	¿No miras que ya el sol sale,	
	y que podrán conocerte	
	desta suerte?	

Sale Coquín.

COQUÍN	Aunque me mates,	
	habiéndote conocido,	
	o señor, tengo de hablarte:	2725
	escúchame.	
REY	Pues, Coquín,	
	¿de qué los extremos son?	
COQUÍN	Ésta es una honrada acción	
	de hombre bien nacido, en fin;	
	que aunque hombre me consideras	2730
	de burlas, con loco humor,	
	llegando a veras, señor,	
	soy hombre de muchas veras.	
	Oye lo que he de decir,	
	pues de veras vengo a hablar;	2735
	que quiero hacerte llorar,	
	ya que no puedo reír.	

and take this diamond. If you show it, they'll allow you to see
me, no matter what time it is.

LUDOVICO   Sir, may heaven keep you safe.

He leaves.

KING   Let's go, Don Diego.

DON DIEGO   What was that?

KING   The most remarkable thing in the world.

DON DIEGO   Something has left you sad.

KING   I couldn't help but be astounded.

DON DIEGO   Why don't you go to bed? The day is beginning to show among
the gold-hued clouds.

KING   I won't be able to rest until I find a certain house.

DON DIEGO   Don't you see that the sun's coming up now, and people could
recognize you?

Coquín enters.

COQUÍN   Oh, sir, although you may kill me because I've recognized you,
I must speak with you: please listen to me.

KING   Well, Coquín, why all the fuss?

COQUÍN   This is an honourable action by a man who is, after all is said
and done, well born. Because although you consider me a
silly jester, when it comes right down to it, sir, I am a man of
considerable truth. Listen to what I have to say, because I really
need to speak with you. Since I cannot make you laugh, I wish
to make you weep.

2714 **Something has left you sad:** We have seen similar phrasing in Act I, in Jacinta's
comment to Doña Mencía after the Prince's departure from the country home (line 555).

2730–3 *hombre ... de burlas*: see lines 2375–6 note. On *hombre de ... veras*: 'Man of truth.
He who by nature, mind or behaviour is a friend of reality and truth: or he is serious, and an
enemy of foolishness' (*Autoridades*, III, p. 457b). *Hombre de muchas veras* may also mean
'very much a man'.

2736–7 **Since I can't make you laugh, I wish to make you weep:** Alternatively, '[S]ince I
can no longer laugh, I wish to make you weep'.

Gutierre, mal informado
por aparentes recelos,
llegó a tener viles celos   2740
de su honor; y hoy, obligado
    a tal sospecha, que halló
escribiendo (¡error cruel!)
para el Infante un papel
a su esposa que intentó   2745
    con él que no se ausentase,
porque ella causa no fuese
de que en Sevilla se viese
la novedad que causase
    pensar que ella le ausentaba…   2750
con esta inocencia pues
(que a mí consta), con pies
cobardes, adonde estaba
    llegó, y el papel tomó,
y, sus celos declarados,   2755
despidiendo a los criados,
todas las puertas cerró,
    solo se quedó con ella.
Yo, enternecido de ver
una infelice mujer,   2760
perseguida de su estrella,
    vengo, señor, a avisarte
que tu brazo altivo y fuerte
hoy la libre de la muerte.

REY   ¿Con qué he de poder pagarte   2765
                   tal piedad?

COQUÍN   Con darme aprisa
               libre, sin más accidentes,
               de la acción contra mis dientes.

REY   No es ahora tiempo de risa.

COQUÍN   ¿Cuándo lo fue?

REY   Y pues el día   2770
               aun no se muestra, lleguemos,
               don Diego. Así, pues, daremos
               color a una industria mía,
                   de entrar en casa mejor,
               diciendo que me ha cogido   2775
               el día cerca, y he querido

Gutierre, led astray by unfounded jealousy, became very suspicious about his honour. Today, driven by this suspicion, he found his wife writing to the Prince not to leave Seville – oh, what a cruel mistake! She didn't want people to think Enrique left because of her. Although I can vouch for her innocence, consumed by jealousy, Gutierre crept up on her, took the paper, dismissed all the servants, and remained alone in the house with her. Today I come, sir, out of pity for this unhappy woman, persecuted by fate, to ask that with your proud and mighty power you save her from death.

KING   How can I reward such compassion?

COQUÍN By immediately and without any delay releasing me from the contract on my teeth.

KING   Now is not the time for laughter.

COQUÍN When was it ever?

KING   Don Diego, since the sun hasn't risen yet, let's go. I have a plan to go to a certain wealthy house, saying that the day has caught me

	disimular el color
	del vestido; y una vez
	allá, el estado veremos
	del suceso; y así haremos 2780
	como Rey, Supremo Juez.
DON DIEGO	No hubiera industria mejor.
COQUÍN	De su casa lo has tratado
	tan cerca, que ya has llegado;
	que ésta es su casa, señor. 2785
REY	Don Diego, espera.
DON DIEGO	¿Qué ves?
REY	¿No ves sangrienta una mano
	impresa en la puerta?
DON DIEGO	Es llano.
REY	[*Ap.*] Gutierre sin duda es
	el cruel que anoche hizo 2790
	una acción tan inclemente.
	No sé hacer; cuerdamente
	sus agravios satisfizo.

Salen doña Leonor y [Inés], criada.

DOÑA LEONOR	Salgo a misa antes del día,
	porque ninguno me vea 2795
	en Sevilla, donde crea
	que olvido la pena mía.
	Mas gente hay aquí. ¡Ay, Inés!
	¿El Rey qué hará en esta casa?
INÉS	Tápate en tanto que pasa. 2800
REY	Acción excusada es,
	porque ya estáis conocida.
DOÑA LEONOR	No fue encubrirme, señor,
	por excusar el honor
	de dar a tus pies la vida. 2805
REY	Esa acción es para mí,
	de recatarme de vos,
	pues sois acreedor, por Dios,
	de mis honras; que yo os di
	palabra, y con gran razón, 2810
	de que he de satisfacer
	vuestro honor; y lo he de hacer
	en la primera ocasión.

	nearby, and that I need to change my red cloak. Once there, we'll see how the matter stands, and then we'll perform as King, the Supreme Judge.
DON DIEGO	There couldn't be a better plan.
COQUÍN	Since we weren't far from the house already, sir, here it is.
KING	Don Diego, wait.
DON DIEGO	What is it?
KING	Don't you see a bloody handprint on the door?
DON DIEGO	It's clear.
KING	[*Aside*] Gutierre must be the cruel man who performed such a merciless deed last night. I don't know what to do; he's avenged his honour in a most cunning way.

Doña Leonor and [Inés], a maid, enter.

DA. LEONOR	I'm going to mass before dawn, so that no one in Seville will see me and think I forget my grievance.
	But people are here. Oh, Inés! What can the King be doing at this house?
INÉS	Cover your face while he passes by.
KING	There's no point, because I already know who you are.
DA. LEONOR	Sir, I wasn't trying to avoid paying you my respects.
KING	By heaven, it is I who should be shrinking from you, because I owe you the restoration of your honour. I gave you my word, and with good reason, that I would satisfy your honour, and that I'll do at the first opportunity.

Don Gutierre, dentro.

DON GUTIERRE	Hoy me he de desesperar,
	cielo cruel, si no baja
	un rayo de esas esferas,
	y en cenizas me desata.
REY	¿Qué es esto?
DON DIEGO	Loco furioso
	don Gutierre de su casa
	sale.

2815

[Sale don Gutierre.]

REY	¿Dónde vais, Gutierre?
DON GUTIERRE	A besar, señor, tus plantas;
	y de la mayor desdicha,
	de la tragedia más rara,
	escucha la admiración
	que eleva, admira y espanta.
	Mencía, mi amada esposa,
	tan hermosa como casta,
	virtuosa como bella
	(dígalo a voces la fama):
	Mencía, a quien adoré
	con la vida y con el alma,
	anoche a un grave accidente
	vio su perfección postrada,
	por desmentirla divina
	este accidente de humana.
	Un médico, que lo es
	el de mayor nombre y fama,
	y el que en el mundo merece
	inmortales alabanzas,
	la recetó una sangría,
	porque con ella esperaba
	restituir la salud
	a un mal de tanta importancia.
	Sangróse en fin; que yo mismo,
	por estar sola la casa,
	llamé el barbero, no habiendo
	ni criados ni criadas.
	A verla en su cuarto, pues,
	quise entrar esta mañana

2820

2825

2830

2835

2840

2845

Don Gutierre, from within.

DON GUTIERRE   Cruel heavens, I'm going to kill myself, if you don't cast down a lightning bolt to strike me dead today.

KING   What's this?

DON DIEGO   Don Gutierre is coming out of his house in a frenzy.

[Don Gutierre enters.]

KING   Where are you going, Gutierre?

DON GUTIERRE   To pay you my respects, sir. And now listen to the strangest tragedy: the most extraordinary and astonishing thing has happened.

Mencía, my beloved wife, as beautiful as she was chaste, as virtuous as she was lovely (her reputation proves it): Mencía, whom I adored with my life and soul, saw her perfection laid low last night by a grievous mortal accident, this human accident belying her divinity.

An illustrious physician, a man of the greatest reputation, prescribed for her a bloodletting. He hoped to cure a very dangerous illness. So she was bled; because the house was deserted, all the servants gone, I myself called the barber.·

This morning I went to see her in her room. Now I can't

2814   *desesperarse*: 'To kill oneself by any means out of despair; a sin against the Holy Spirit ...' (Covarrubias, p. 414a).
2819+   [*Sale don Gutierre*] / [*Don Gutierre enters.*] We have added this stage direction.
2844–6 So she was bled; ... called the barber: See line 2585 note.

(aquí la lengua enmudece,   2850
aquí el aliento me falta);
veo de funesta sangre
teñida toda la cama,
toda la ropa cubierta,
y que en ella, ¡ay Dios!, estaba   2855
Mencía, que se había muerto
esta noche desangrada.
Ya se ve cuán fácilmente
una venda se desata.
¿Pero para qué presumo   2860
reducir hoy a palabras
tan lastimosas desdichas?
Vuelve a esta parte la cara,
y verás sangriento el sol,
verás la luna eclipsada,   2865
deslucidas las estrellas,
y las esferas borradas;
y verás a la hermosura
más triste y más desdichada,
que por darme mayor muerte,   2870
no me ha dejado sin alma.

Descubre a doña Mencía en una cama, desangrada.

REY   ¡Notable sujeto! ([*Ap.*] Aquí
                 la prudencia es de importancia:
                 mucho en reportarme haré:
                 tomó notable venganza.)   2875
                 Cubrid ese horror que asombra,
                 ese prodigio que espanta,
                 espectáculo que admira,
                 símbolo de la desgracia.
                 Gutierre, menester es   2880
                 consuelo; y porque la haya
                 en pérdida que es tan grande,
                 con otra tanta ganancia,
                 dadle la mano a Leonor;
                 que es tiempo que satisfaga   2885

speak, I can't breathe. I saw the whole bed drenched in awful
blood, all the covers soaked, and Mencía was – Oh God! – in
the bed. During the night she died, from loss of blood. Now we
see how easily a bandage comes loose.

But how can I put such a catastrophe into words? Turn your
gaze in this direction, and you'll see the sun bloodied, you'll
see the moon eclipsed, the stars drained of light, and the spheres
obliterated. You'll see the saddest and most wretched beauty,
whose dying brings death to me, leaving my soul behind to
suffer.

He reveals Doña Mencía in a bed, drained of blood.

KING   A remarkable subject! ([*Aside*] Here I must be prudent; I've got
                 to show restraint: he took a remarkable revenge.)

                 Cover up that shocking horror, that monstrous wonder, that
                 amazing spectacle, symbol of calamity.

                 Gutierre, you need consolation. Since your loss is so terrible,
                 for a gain just as great, give your hand to Leonor: it's time for

---

2871+   He reveals Doña Mencía ...: Here Don Gutierre may for the third time (see lines
1896+ and 2457+ notes) draw open the curtain of the middle door at the back of the stage,
on this occasion revealing Doña Mencía's body in the bed. This is one of the most famous
'scenes of horror' in the Spanish Golden Age *comedia*.
  Amezcua (pp. 85–87) has discussed what he considers to be a spatial anomaly in Calderón's
design of this scene. While the King, Don Diego, Doña Leonor, Inés, and Coquín meet
Don Gutierre outside his house, where they see the bloody handprint, in order to discover
Doña Mencía's body in her bedroom, Calderón must have brought them inside the house.
Nevertheless, no stage direction or dialogue indicates the group's movement. Amezcua
believes to be symbolic what may be a deliberate omission on the playwright's part: Don
Gutierre's private home has become as public and degraded as the streets of Seville. On
staging this scene, see Cruickshank 2003, p. 31.
2872   ¡*Notable sujeto!* / A remarkable subject!: Among the meanings of *sujeto* (subject) are
'the person of special quality or talents.... It also means the material, subject, or theme about
which one speaks or writes' (*Autoridades*, III, p. 181a). In the *Diccionario crítico etimológico
de la lengua castellana*, IV, p. 293b, under the entry *súdito* – which in *Autoridades* (III,
p.167[a]) and today means political subject – Joan Corominas quotes Antonio de Nebrija in the
Dictionarium ex hispaniensi in latinum sermonem (1493 or 1495) as indicating that *súdito*
and *sujeto* are interchangeable, both being derived from the Latin *subditus*. Therefore, the
King may be remarking on the subject matter; on Gutierre as a political subject; and/or on
Gutierre as a 'person of special quality or talents'.

vuestro valor lo que debe,
y yo cumpla la palabra
de volver en la ocasión
por su valor y su fama.

DON GUTIERRE Señor, si de tanto fuego   2890
aún las cenizas se hallan
calientes, dadme lugar
para que llore mis ansias.
¿No queréis que escarmentado
quede?

REY   Esto ha de ser, y basta.   2895

DON GUTIERRE Señor, ¿queréis que otra vez,
no libre de la borrasca,
vuelva al mar? ¿Con qué disculpa?

REY Con que vuestro Rey lo manda.

DON GUTIERRE Señor, escuchad aparte   2900
disculpas.

REY   Son excusadas.
¿Cuáles son?

DON GUTIERRE   ¿Si vuelvo a verme
en desdichas tan extrañas,
que de noche halle embozado
a vuestro hermano en mi casa?   2905

REY No dar crédito a sospechas.

DON GUTIERRE ¿Y si detrás de mi cama
hallase tal vez, señor,
de don Enrique la daga?

REY Presumir que hay en el mundo   2910
mil sobornadas criadas,
y apelar a la cordura.

DON GUTIERRE A veces, señor, no basta.
¿Si veo rondar después
de noche y de día mi casa?   2915

REY Quejárseme a mí.

DON GUTIERRE   ¿Y si cuando
llego a quejarme, me aguarda
mayor desdicha escuchando?

REY ¿Qué importa si él desengaña,
que fue siempre su hermosura   2920
una constante muralla,
de los vientos defendida?

	you as a noble man to satisfy your debt; and for me to fulfill my word that I would see to her good name.
DON GUTIERRE	Sir, if the ashes from so much fire are still warm, give me time to grieve. Don't you want me to learn from my painful experience?
KING	I command it, and that's enough.
DON GUTIERRE	Sir, do you want me to return to the sea while the storm still rages? Why?
KING	Your King commands it.
DON GUTIERRE	Sir, listen to my excuses in private.
KING	There's no point. What are they?
DON GUTIERRE	What if I find myself again in such strange circumstances that I discover your brother hiding in my house?
KING	Don't believe your suspicions.
DON GUTIERRE	And if perhaps behind my bed I find Don Enrique's dagger?
KING	Assume that maids are bribed every day, and use your good sense.
DON GUTIERRE	Sometimes that's not enough, sir. What if after that, I see him prowling around on my street, day and night?
KING	Complain to me.
DON GUTIERRE	And when I do come to complain, what if I hear something even worse?
KING	What difference does it make, if he reveals the truth: this beauty was always faithful, like a wall against the winds?

DON GUTIERRE	¿Y si volviendo a mi casa
	hallo algún papel que pide
	que el Infante no se vaya?

2925

REY	Para todo habrá remedio.
DON GUTIERRE	¿Posible es que a esto le haya?
REY	Sí, Gutierre.
DON GUTIERRE	¿Cuál, señor?
REY	Uno vuestro.
DON GUTIERRE	¿Qué es?
REY	Sangralla.
DON GUTIERRE	¿Qué decís?
REY	Que hagáis borrar

2930

las puertas de vuestra casa;
que hay mano sangrienta en ella.

DON GUTIERRE Los que de un oficio tratan,
ponen, señor, a las puertas
un escudo de sus armas: 2935
trato en honor, y así pongo
mi mano en sangre bañada
a la puerta; que el honor
con sangre, señor, se lava.

REY   Dádsela, pues, a Leonor,   2940
que yo sé que su alabanza
la merece.

DON GUTIERRE   Sí la doy.
Mas mira, que va bañada
en sangre, Leonor.

DOÑA LEONOR   No importa;
que no me admira ni espanta.   2945

DON GUTIERRE Mira que médico he sido
de mi honra: no está olvidada
la ciencia.

DOÑA LEONOR   Cura con ella
mi vida, en estando mala.

DON GUTIERRE Pues con esa condición   2950
te la doy. Con esto acaba
el Médico de su honra.
Perdonad sus muchas faltas.

DON GUTIERRE	And if I return to my house to find a letter asking the Prince not to leave?
KING	There is a remedy for everything.
DON GUTIERRE	Could there be one for this?
KING	Yes, Gutierre.
DON GUTIERRE	What is it, sir?
KING	One of yours.
DON GUTIERRE	What's that?
KING	Bleed her.
DON GUTIERRE	What?
KING	Have your doors wiped clean; there's a bloody hand on your house.
DON GUTIERRE	Sir, those who practice a profession put a coat of arms on their doors. I deal in honour, and so I put my bloody hand on the door, because a man's honour can be washed clean with blood.
KING	Then give your hand to Leonor, because I know her excellent reputation deserves it.
DON GUTIERRE	Yes, I will. But look, Leonor, it comes bathed in blood.
DA. LEONOR	It doesn't matter; that doesn't bother me.
DON GUTIERRE	Keep in mind that I've been the physician of my honour, and my science is not forgotten.
DA. LEONOR	Cure me with it, should I become ill.
DON GUTIERRE	Well, on that condition I give it to you. And here *The Physician of His Honour* ends. Pardon its many faults.

2951–3 And here *The Physician of His Honour* ends. Pardon its many faults: The dramatic epilogue was a time-honoured device in European drama, going back at least as far as the *vos plaudite*! ('Now let us hear you applauding!') of Roman drama Horace describes in his *Art of Poetry*, line 155 (see Horace, note p. 374). A character in the play ruptures the dramatic illusion by turning to the audience to request its indulgence or beg its applause. An example in Shakespeare is Rosalind's speech beginning 'It is not the fashion to see the lady [in] the epilogue ...' at the conclusion of *As You Like It*.

In *The Physician of His Honour*, Don Gutierre's final line is ambiguous and could be translated, 'Pardon *his* many faults'. Wardropper writes, 'In plays whose title designates the character, the audience is often beseeched simultaneously to forgive the defects of the play and the errors of the designated character. This ambivalence is particularly evident in wife-murder plays.... [In *The Physician of His Honour*] both the play and the protagonist who imaged himself the surgeon of his honour need to be forgiven' (1986, p. 215).

APPENDIX

HONOR AND *HONRA* IN *THE PHYSICIAN OF HIS HONOUR*

The English word 'honour' is usually rendered by either of two Spanish words, *honor* or *honra*. While the meaning of the words may have been distinguishable in Calderón's time,[1] they overlap a great deal in *The Physician*: at certain points either is used to mean 'public reputation', and at other points either one signifies 'personal integrity'.

However, despite the appearance of *honra* in the title, Calderón uses *honor* far more frequently in the play proper. In Act One, *honor* appears almost exclusively, and refers with few exceptions to the honour of the women Mencía and Leonor. In Act Two, when Gutierre begins to contemplate the condition of his own honour, in asides and soliloquies he addresses *honor* as if it were a person. For example:

---

1   The evidence is murky. *Honor*, in the definitions offered by the first official dictionary of the Spanish language, the *Diccionario de Autoridades* (1724), appears to stress the public attribute corresponding with 'good name' or 'reputation' in English ('It is often taken for illustrious reputation of a family, action, or other thing. It is also taken for praise, applause or celebrity of something. It also means honesty and modesty in women' [Se toma muchas veces por reputación y lustre de alguna familia, acción u otra cosa.... Se toma asimismo por obsequio, apláuso o celebridad de alguna cosa. Significa tambien la honestidad y recato en las mujeres (II, p. 173a)]). In *The Physician*, on several occasions characters in the play use *fama* or *opinión* to convey 'reputation' (see line 847, for example).

Honra, while interchangeable with *honor* in many regards, has been said to impart 'honour' with a more interior connotation, as in 'respect for personal worth' ('Reverence, respect, and veneration that is accorded to virtue, authority, or superiority of some person. It also means point of honour, esteem and good reputation that is found and ought to be maintained in the subject.... It is also the virginal integrity of women' [Reverencia, acatamiento y veneración que se hace à la virtud, autoridad, ò mayoría de alguna persona.... Significa tambien pundonor, estimacion y buena fama, que se halla en el sugeto y debe conservar.... Se toma tambien por la integridad virginal en las mugéres (*Autoridades*, II, p. 173b)]).

Américo Castro, writing in 1961, attempted to clarify the difference between the two as follows: 'The [Spanish] language distinguished the ideal and objective notion of "honor", and the functioning of that same notion, vitally realized in an individualized life's process. "Honor" *is*, but "honra" belongs to someone, it acts and is moving in a life' (El idioma distinguía entre la noción ideal y objetiva del 'honor', y el funcionamiento de esa misma noción, vitalmente realizada en un proceso de vida singularizada. El honor *es*, pero la honra pertenece a alguien, actúa y se está moviendo en una vida [1961, p. 55]).

¡Ay, honor! mucho tenemos	Oh, honour! The two of us have
que hablar a solas los dos… (1401–2)	much to discuss in private…
A peligro estáis, honor… (1659)	Honour, you are in danger…
[O]s he de curar, honor… (1666)	[H]onour, I've got to cure you…

Although Gutierre calls himself 'el médico de su honra' (the physician of his honour, 1673), and proclaims that 'médico de mi honra / me llamo' (I call myself the physician of my honour, 1871–72), he also alludes to himself as 'el médico de honor' (the physician of honour, 1712). In Act Three, Gutierre again uses *honor* far more frequently than *honra*, and if as the play approaches its dénouement he claims that 'médico he sido / de mi honra' (I've been the physician of my honour, 2947), he has earlier proclaimed that 'médico soy de mi honor' (I am the physician of my honour, 2630). The King also observes to Gutierre that 'de vuestro honor / médico os llamáis' (you call yourself the physician of your honour, 2141).

Honra is invoked, then, with relative infrequency, and usually as a synonym for *honor*. Calderón likely made use of the former for variety, and for purposes of rhyme and rhythm, *honra* being stressed on the first syllable, and *honor* on the second.

However, Gutierre's direct address of the masculine *honor* in soliloquies may also show a gendered solidarity between male physician and male patient ('mi enfermo'). And the sparing use of *honra* may also emphasize an ironic implication of which the characters may sometimes but not always be aware. In Spanish, variations on the noun 'honour'—honourable, honoured, to honour; dishonourable, dishonoured, to dishonour—nearly always derive from *honrar* rather than the much rarer *honorar*.[2] In Act One, Gutierre says to Prince Enrique, who the audience already knows is a menace to Mencía's and hence also her husband's honour, 'Honrad por tan breve espacio / esta esfera' ([H]onour my sphere for a time, however brief, 335–36), and, a little later, 'Sabe tu Alteza / honrar' (Your Highness honours me, 350). In act Two Gutierre, now engulfed in suspicions, again addresses the Prince: 'El honrar es dado a vos' (You honour us, 1532); and 'Pienso que me honraréis / tanto, que de mí creeréis / lo que de mí estáis seguro' ([y]ou'll see that honouring me so much will prove wise, 1552–4). That is, with first unwitting and then intended irony on Gutierre's part, when *honrar* is spoken, dishonour is implied.

---

2   Corresponding derivations of 'honor' are rare in Spanish of any period, and nonexistent in *The Physician*.